THE SPIRIT
of PREGNANCY

An Interactive Anthology
for Your Journey to Motherhood

BONNI GOLDBERG

CB
CONTEMPORARY BOOKS

Library of Congress Cataloging-in-Publication Data

Goldberg, Bonni.
    The spirit of pregnancy : an interactive anthology for your journey to
motherhood / Bonni Goldberg.
        p.   cm.
    Includes bibliographical references.
    ISBN 0-8092-2615-4
    1. Pregnancy Popular works.   2. Pregnant women—Psychological
aspects.   3. Motherhood Popular works.   I. Title.   II. Title: Interactive
anthology for your journey to motherhood.
RG525.G51378   2000
618.2′4—dc21   99-38815
                                              CIP

Cover design by Monica Baziuk
Cover photograph copyright © David Perry/Photonica
Interior design by Amy Yu Ng

Published by Contemporary Books
A division of NTC/Contemporary Publishing Group, Inc.
4255 West Touhy Avenue, Lincolnwood (Chicago), Illinois 60712-1975 U.S.A.
Printed in the United States of America
International Standard Book Number: 0-8092-2615-4

00 01 02 03 04 05 MV 19 18 17 16 15 14 13 12 11 10 9 8 7 6 5 4 3 2 1

for Isabel May Rose
who made me a mother

Other books by Bonni Goldberg:

Room to Write: Daily Invitations to a Writer's Life

Gifts from the Heart: Meditations on Caring for Aging Parents (with Geo Kendall)

Contents

Credits

Acknowledgments

*I*f it takes a village to raise a child, it took a community, like the one I'm privileged to be a part of, to help me create a book during early motherhood.

I thank my agent, Lisa Swayne, for her vision and support throughout this project and her assistant, Dina DiMaio, without whom I could not have even begun.

At Contemporary Books, I want to thank Kara Leverte for continuing to champion my dreams and for giving me the extra time I needed and Susan Moore-Kruse for making the production process smooth.

For the emergency technical support, I thank Jon Timian, Lisa Lewenz, Julia Peattie, and Gary Beaver.

I am indebted to the wonderful Multnomah County Public Library system, particularly the Belmont branch, and especially Alison Kastner.

I want to thank all the moms and babies that took turns spending time with Isabel while I worked: Patty Ryan and Katherine, Devorah Spilman and Hannah, Amy Corneliussen and Rain, Julie Haun and Isaac, Dona Manning and Timber, Sister Bragdon and Jane.

It has been a great pleasure and honor to extend my community through coming to know the writers-mothers who have contributed to this collection.

Though it goes without saying, I will say it anyway: my greatest thanks goes to my spouse, Geo Kendall, my total partner in creation, be it child, marriage, or dreams come true.

The womb is like an animal within an animal.
—*Aretaeus*

※

coil like a serpent
sleep like a lamb
—*inscribed on a gold amulet, Kiev, 11th century*
prayer to the womb for women's fertility

Introduction

*I*f you are pregnant, you are in the midst of a rich, mysterious, and enlightening period of your life: an odyssey and metamorphosis all in one. Much as there is to learn about your body, your baby, and your hormones, there is also a great deal to glean about the person you are becoming—the new identity you are incorporating into your former self. In contemporary life, many of us live at a pace so divided from the rhythms that create and sustain the natural world that it is possible to lose touch with the importance of this ageless transformation, this time spent in the liminal world.

Pregnancy is an initiation, a rite of passage. When a baby is born, so is a mother. Women experience the nine months of gestation so differently because each of us needs a particular set of circumstances to prepare us to mother. Even if you're already a mother, as Suzy Vitello's "Dancing with the Paper Rose" points out, each pregnancy offers new insights.

I had imagined being pregnant as a means to an end. I thought giving birth was the start of the life-altering journey of motherhood. But that journey had already begun from the moment I suspected I was pregnant. I was told it takes nine months to grow a baby because women need the time to prepare for motherhood. Almost every aspect of my pregnancy, the joys and the trials, also *gave* me something I needed to experience within myself to be a mother.

Into my second trimester, I became frustrated reading pregnancy guides. I couldn't access the wisdom I needed from information about my body or about "the growth of the fetus." I put those manuals aside awhile and went to the place humanity keeps its most important truths: literature. I searched the library. I knew that if I was in the middle of a timeless, epic journey, and not just preparing for it, the stories, poems, and narratives of those before me would be there like lighthouses to guide me along the way. And they were.

It's surprising how much we can discover when we return to events through literature, and it's never too late to gain insight from a rite of passage. The selected poems, essays, and stories in this collection are the voices of those before you: the tongues of the bells sounding concerns and themes that are a part of the initiation of pregnancy.

When I finished Anne Lamott's "Some Thoughts on Being Pregnant," it confirmed how conflicted I felt about mothering. After putting down Molly Giles's "Baby Pictures," I was able to put into words the shift already taking place in my relationship to my work. Reading Louise Erdrich I felt my own growing sense of strength and vulnerability. Though some of what I read didn't directly relate to my circumstances, each piece brought up something that helped me sort through my thoughts and emotions during this transformative time.

These voices weren't always easy to find. Birth and new motherhood dominated most collections. In the drama of those experiences do we forget all that transpires in the timeless months of gestation? Why isn't there a collection just about pregnancy? I complained to my spouse and then my agent. Make one, they replied. So I created the book I wished had been there for me. I gathered some of the writings I had discovered while pregnant and invited other writers to add their voices. The result is this anthology.

I decided to include another item I wished for as well: a place to record what was happening to my psyche. Even though I'm a writer, I didn't feel like writing much while pregnant. An artist I know admitted she didn't paint a single piece during her pregnancy because she felt so complete. I wanted a no-pressure opportunity to keep track of my impressions and insights—nothing as vast as a whole blank journal, which I was sure to misplace as I became increasingly absent-minded (a phenomenon one friend calls "pregnant brain")—just a page or two for between naps or during night wakings. I hope these pages become a resource for you and perhaps someday for your children.

By the time labor began, I was already a mother; as fledgling and newborn as my infant daughter, but still a mother. Not because I was overcome with a wave of maternal instinct, but because during pregnancy I uncovered new aspects of myself, let go of others, and most important, came to accept parts of myself my child and I would have to live with. Three months of 24-hour morning sickness assured me I could put aside my plans and desires without losing my identity. Feeling my little one tumble and kick inside helped me let go of a tired, old image I had of myself as empty. Living through the consequences of a less than perfect sonogram propelled me into acceptance of my propensity toward anxiety and the commitment I made to manage it differently for the sake of my daughter and myself. Despite how utterly pregnancy altered me physically, I changed most inside myself, and those changes were the significant and lasting ones.

Pregnancy changed and challenged me and made me feel twice born. It altered as many beliefs as it confirmed about the core of who I am. This inner renovation created room for the new aspect of my identity—mother of Isabel. It also helped me embrace faith—not the everything-will-be-OK brand, but a trust in the intelligence of change: faith in place of hope.

How to Use This Book

The blank pages that follow each piece of writing are for you to record what resonates for you: how you feel about the subject matter as it relates to your own pregnancy. The prompts included are my suggestions for exploring, examining, and learning from your pregnancy. If different aspects of the piece you've read speak to you, put mine aside and speak to yours. Whether you read the forty pieces in order or skip around, you will be glad if you date each of your entries in the space provided. You might respond to the readings through drawing, collage, or other creative modes. If you use writing, any form is fine: journaling; poetry; lists; a story; notes to yourself, your baby, or someone else; a series of letters. If you have friends who are also pregnant, consider joining together to talk about the readings and your responses. Even friends or relatives who have already had their children can participate with you as a way to touch the richness of their pregnancies in retrospect. To embrace and take full advantage of the incredible experience of pregnancy, you only have to be open, listen, and add *your* voice.

May 1968

Sharon Olds

The Dean of the University said
the neighborhood people could not cross campus
until the students gave up the buildings
so we lay down in the street,
we said The cops will enter this gate
over our bodies. Spine-down on the cobbles—
hard bed, like a carton of eggs—
I saw the buildings of New York City
from dirt level, they soared up and stopped,
chopped off cleanly—beyond them the sky
black and neither sour nor sweet, the
night air over the island.
The mounted police moved near us
delicately. Flat out on our backs
we sang, and then I began to count,
12, 13, 14, 15, I
counted again, 15, 16, one
month since the day on that deserted beach when we
used nothing, 17, 18, my
mouth fell open, my hair in the soil,
if my period did not come tonight
I was pregnant. I looked up at the sole of the
cop's shoe, I looked up at the
horse's belly, its genitals—if they
took me to Women's Detention and did the

exam on me, jammed the unwashed
speculum high inside me, the guard's
three fingers—supine on Broadway, I looked
up into the horse's tail like a
dark filthed comet. All week, I had
wanted to get arrested, longed to
give myself away. I lay in the
tar, one brain in my head and another
tiny brain at the base of my tail and I
stared at the world, good-luck iron
arc of the gelding's shoe, the cop's
baton, the deep curve of the animal's
belly, the buildings streaming up
away from the earth. I knew I should get up and
leave, stand up to muzzle level, to the
height of the soft velvet nostrils and
walk away, turn my back on my
friends and danger, but I was a coward so I
lay there looking up at the sky,
black vault arched above us, I
lay there gazing up at God, at his
underbelly, till it turned deep blue and then
silvery, colorless, *Give me this one
night*, I said, *and I'll give this child
the rest of my life*, the horses' heads
drooping, dipping, until they slept in a
dark circle around my body and my daughter. ❧

Describe when you realized you were pregnant. What were you in the middle of? What did you want one more day, week, month, year for?

Date _____

Excerpts from *The Blue Jay's Dance*

Louise Erdrich

From: December. Deep snow and middle trimester. Where I work.

I come here every day to work, starting while invisibly pregnant. I imagine myself somewhere else, into another skin, another person, another time. Yet simultaneously my body is constructing its own character. It requires no thought at all for me to form and fix a whole other person. First she is nothing, then she is growing and dividing at such a rate I think I'll drop. I come in eager hope and afraid of labor, all at once, for this is the heart of the matter. Whatever else I do, when it comes to pregnancy I am my physical self first, as are all of us women. We can pump gas, lift weights, head a corporation, lead nations, and tune pianos. Still, our bodies are rounded vases of skin and bones and blood that seem impossibly engineered for birth. I look down onto my smooth, huge lap, feel my baby twist, and I can't figure out how I'll ever stretch wide enough. I fear I've made a ship inside a bottle. I'll have to break. I'm not me. I feel myself becoming less a person than a place, inhabited, a foreign land. I will experience pain, lose physical control, or know the uncertainty of anesthetic. I fear these things, but vaguely, for my brain buzzes in the merciful wash of endorphins that preclude any thought from occupying it too long. Most of all, I worry over what I hold. I want perfection. Each day I pray another perfect cell to form. A million of them. I fear that my tears, my moods, my wrenched weeping will imprint on the baby's psyche. I fear repression, a stoic face shown to the world, will cause our child to hide emotions. I make too much of myself, expect too many favors, or not enough. I rock and rock and stare out the window into my life.

Advice

Most of the instruction given to pregnant women is as chirpy and condescending as the usual run of maternity clothes—the wide tops with droopy bows slung beneath the neck, the T-shirts with arrows pointing to what can't be missed, the childish sailor collars, puffed sleeves, and pastels. It is cute advice—what to pack in the hospital bag (don't forget a toothbrush, deodorant, a comb or hair dryer)—or it's worse: pseudo-spiritual, misleading, silly, and even cruel. In giving birth to three daughters, I have found it impossible to eliminate pain through breathing, by focusing on a soothing photograph. It is true *pain* one is attempting to endure in drugless labor, not "discomfort," and the way to deal with pain is not to call it something else but to increase in strength, to prepare the will. Women are strong, strong, terribly strong. We don't know how strong we are until we're pushing out our babies. We are too often treated like babies having babies when we should be in training, like acolytes, novices to high priestess-hood, like serious applicants for the space program.

January. Sweet hopes and poker hands.

The blueprint for all our inherited characteristics is provided by the DNA molecules in the nuclei of our cells. The entire structure is composed of roughly three billion such pairs, together making up 100,000 genes. It is thrilling, dizzying, to consider the order of these pairs in the human genome, the total genetic message. Staring into my lap, I imagine genes shuffling together like poker hands and my thoughts swim toward stacked, incalculable numbers.

When we make love in the darkness of anticipation we are inviting accident and order, the careful lining up of genes. Unlocking the components of another person, we are safecrackers—setting the combinations, unconsciously twirling dials. Shadow brothers, sisters, potential unfused others, cease. Our children grow into existence particularized, yet random.

Eating

It isn't just eating, of course, and there's the joy. Now it's even better, for I never know which bite is destined for the heart, the muscles, hair, the bones forming like the stalks of flowers, or the lovely eyes. Michael makes Jell-O for me so that the baby will have perfect fingernails. He attempts, in his cooking, to get every part of the baby right. Of course, the real challenge in the beginning of pregnancy is how to find exactly what food is bearable in the clutch of morning sickness.

Sleep is the only truly palatable food at first. I sleep hungrily, angry, needy for sleep, jealous for sleep, devouring it and yet resentful of the time it takes away from conscious life. I dream crazily, powerfully. I catch touchdown passes for the Vikings, incite the jealousy of Princess Di, talk earnestly and intimately with a huge male Kodiak brown bear, fly headlong over these low northeastern mountains. Morning comes. I throw up quickly, efficiently, miserably, and eat a cracker. It does no good at all to fight the feeling. For garden-variety morning sickness, which is all I've ever had, not the serious kind that requires hospitalization, very little can be done except to endure. I am not an advice giver, but I will offer these helpful strategies. When very sick, plain saltines are the best. They are an everyday cracker, though, and one should watch for sales on expensive English water biscuits—something special for the weekends. Plain low-salt wheat thins, Stoned Wheat Thins, mild Cheddar Goldfish crackers, Bremner Wafers, and an occasional cardboard Finland toast make you feel ascetic, balanced. I eat matzos in great tiles and sheets. A meal of croissant crackers and ginger ale drunk from Michael's grandmother's wineglass is both mournful and restorative. The perfect love-gift for this delicate time? A box of Carr's assorted crackers, all of which come in complex toasted shapes, so that you can pretend you are actually eating a variety of foods.

Around month four, if you are fortunate, when you can eat any food and have a roaring appetite, try something intense—say, a food associated with a first love affair, provided you regard it now with nostalgic joy and are glad it's finished. A jar of bittersweet chocolate syrup, perhaps, only to be licked from a bare finger. These next few months are the most sensuous and sexual of your life—you're not too big and your baby's not in the way and your breasts are stunning creatures right from the Song of Solomon.

You will need every resource.

Perhaps you didn't eat during your fateful encounters, or cannot remember what, or perhaps your greatest emotions were of the intellect, or perhaps you are a plain eater and never developed the taste for an aphrodisiac before, or you could be having this baby all on your own, for which you should be simply adored. At any rate, just in case, I offer the following possible candidates as the most sensuous of foods—a fresh cold cherry soup made with a little cream and cinnamon. Fry bread cooked small, in new oil, with a dollop of chokecherry jam. Hawaiian kettle-fried potato chips. Flan. Anything barbecued.

TV Dinner

Our house has no pump, but receives its water via gravity from a shallow well uphill which contains, in a wet year, cold, leaf-filtered rainwater that keeps a mineral volume in the mouth, and tastes as though it has run through the roots of birch trees. One morning two pregnancies ago, however, during a drought, I turned the faucet wide and heard the thunk and yawn of air in the pipes. The hollow sound reverberated right through my body, for I knew immediately that the well had gone dry. As we had no money to drill a well, we hauled water for a month, showered in the school gym, and used the thickets and underbrush that stretched for miles around the house.

I don't recommend the experience, but sometimes I think that our baby's emotional wealth and appreciation of the natural world was assisted by the fact that I rose at three each morning to walk out into the night woods. Fireflies throbbed in the heavy blackness, sending out ardent messages. I paused sleepily to watch. Surely our baby heard the thin riffs of crickets that ceased and swelled after my steps, and surely the night oxygen bubbled into her, blood rich, cool, and dark. ❦

What do you dream at night? Has your sense of time changed? How? Reflect on ways you feel invaded by your pregnancy and ways you feel protective toward the presence of life forming. What about food? Describe your former and pregnant relationships to it. How do they speak to the ways you nourish yourself and others?

Date _____

An Unmeasured Thing

Vicki Forman

Rachel's wedding day dawns overcast. Even before she is fully awake, Rachel senses clouds and haze: a dark morning, a day of threatened rain. With her eyes closed, she stretches sleep from her and thinks of what is left to be done, and how strange it is that this is the day, finally, when she will marry Stu. Her nerves have made her wake up early, in a room too gray, and long before she needs to, long before the alarm has sounded. Stu breathes beside her, still asleep, while she lies with her arms flat along her sides, the blanket pulled over her head, afraid, of what she is not sure, of the dark shapes perhaps in the room with her, of the man lying next to her, of how quietly the day begins.

Rachel imagines this day to come, trying to invent reassurance.

She'll stand beside Stu, she thinks, the man whose cleft between his chin matches somehow the dimple at the right side of her smile. This isn't proof they belong together, but an indication at least.

In the white dress she and Rose found among negligees at Sandy's Thrift, a dress stretched across the swell that has started to show along her belly, Rachel will walk up the aisle, up the space really, between borrowed folding chairs. No one can come to the wedding unless they also bring a chair. Rachel sees the faces of these guests urging her forward, watching her and wondering. What was she wearing that was borrowed? What was blue? What was old, what was new?

In the front row, her mother, fresh curls, fresh red hair, is crying.

Because all men—and this comes from experience, mind you, not books—will try to run your life and you're too young to have even an inkling yet of what the life is that he's going to run, drawls Rachel's mother afterward in explanation. Because of these tears and these words, and because she leaves so early, so suddenly, hardly before the party has even started, right after the champagne toast but long before they have cut the cake, Rachel will decide not to tell her mother about the baby.

Rachel imagines that before the first electric chords of the wedding march sound from a borrowed upright organ, she and Stu look at each other, and kiss each other, and embrace each other for the last time as people single, separate and apart. They know they're not supposed to see one another before the wedding, and Stu's brother, Ethan, and his best friends, Rich and Roger, and all sorts of other half-drunk men have tried to keep them apart, have tried to get Stu drunk, have done the groomsmen's job of trying to talk Stu out of it (It's not too late to change your mind, they say, their voices low against their own wives' ears. Look at us, they say, Aren't we warning enough?). But Stu loves Rachel and keeps having to find her every twenty minutes, no matter where she is or what she's doing, to tell her that, to hold her from behind and place his wide hands across her stomach and bend his head to smell the honeysuckle blossom in her hair. She leans into him each time, pressing herself against his size. This last time, before their love march among borrowed chairs, Rachel will turn to trace the lines of Stu's face and attempt to imagine the infant version of these shapes that is inside her, to see what a boy will look like, or a girl, with Stu's cleft or her own dimple. It is a trick she plays so often now, this game of pretend, of groping in the dark for solid shapes and a set of features to give to the thing inside her. Rachel laughs, and her mind comes up empty yet again, and she disappears, her throat catching on a breath, into Stu's embrace.

While the guests shuffle in from the porch, the kitchen, the upstairs, outside, to the living room, while the sun emerges finally from behind a cloud, breaking the sky's stretch of smoke apart with yellow fire, Rachel finds herself alone in the bedroom, crying. She doesn't know why. She thinks it has to do with Rose, whom she sees standing below in her garden, tending in heels and a dress to the mass of weeds they have all let grow there. Under Rose's arm is a bouquet of sunflowers. She has cut down the eight-foot-high plants to make a wedding gift of them to Rachel, and the stalks are so long they trail behind her, making it seem that Rose carries sunflower trees whose tops are as big as her head. They vie for Rachel's attention, these brown seeded faces, pocked by the birds who have raided their surfaces, ringed with huge wilting petals that look like a hundred yellow tongues. Rose carries five of these faces under her right arm. They are her company, her guests. They are taller than Rose, and if she were to stand them upright they would tower over her, tilting their faces down at her to speak. Their leathery green petals are like arms that are flippers and could slap you, but Rose is their friend and they wrap themselves around her in the breeze.

Rachel watches Rose and her sunflowers and is not able to stop the tears from forming, from clinging to her lashes where they feel like rain, like mist, like dew.

It has been a long day already.

It is early afternoon, she imagines, and the rooms downstairs hum.

It is her wedding day, and Stu's.

She watches Rose. She puts a pinkie to each corner of her eye, and one at a time she feels the cold pressure and the release as each tear collected drops to her finger. She will wish she knew why she was crying. It will seem important at this moment, even though later, when she stands with Stu and the last electric strains of the wedding march fade, she will not think of Rose, or the sunflowers, or even her tears, except for the small tightness they leave around her eyes.

Before the trip upstairs to get dressed and ready, before Rose ever gets to the garden, long before Stu's embrace or her tears, there is a list full of activity that prevents Rachel from thinking much about the day, about the potential momentousness of it all. This is fine. No one asks a bride on her wedding day how she feels; the assumption is, this is what she wants.

Odd rumblings will move through her stomach whenever she stops to notice.

At midday, in the empty kitchen, she finds Ethan alone at the back door, moving to hide his first beer of this long day. With full coolers in every room, the temptation has been too great. His hand hangs midair from a nearby shelf and his expression has the static, surprised quality of a person caught. When she moves to stand next to him, Rachel sees on the shelf an amber bottle, label turned away, fresh, cold, a line midway across it where the wet bottle sweat begins. The line tells her Ethan has taken at least two long pulls. Rachel leans toward Ethan, risks an embrace. He tells her how happy he is for her, then pulls open the door to the back steps, hurried, his head down. Someone will call to her, she will leave the kitchen. When she comes back through the swinging kitchen door, her eyes move for a moment to that shelf and an instinct is confirmed. The bottle is gone.

As she is about to enter the kitchen before this exchange, Rachel thinks: I am happy.

And before that. She stands on the front porch, helping Stu weave their wedding garland along the rail. The honeysuckle vine gives off its sap; their hands grow sticky and suddenly bees come to find out about the flowers. Rachel has a fear of bees and steps back on the porch to let Stu finish by himself. Stu works among them, undisturbed, not stopping even to swat, not even once, but working steadily at the unfolding garland that they have woven at night before bed, an unmeasured thing that reaches along the porch rail. Stu stretches it across the entry, like a banner, twisting it back down again to the other side of the railing to find, at the end, that it has fit perfectly. Bees weave themselves among the blossoms, black dots that hang midair, then skim across the leaves to dive, buzzing, onto the flowers. Rachel clutches her arms across her chest, concerned. Will the guests mind, will they risk stepping onto the porch past this curtain of bees? Stu will swear, as he plucks a blossom, waves a bee from it, and puts it in her hair behind her ear, he will swear they will. They surely will, he says, kissing her.

This will be enough, oddly, to make her happy.

Moving steadily through each moment before the last, Rachel finds herself with a cup of coffee, her third, wandering through the field of still-asleep guests who lie across their living room floor. They are late to wake up after the party the night before. She tiptoes past the remains, the full ashtrays and half-empty beer bottles. From the coffee, she feels her stomach begin what will be a day of small burstings. She thinks of her guests, and their headaches, and Rose.

It is the light, she thinks, moving toward the open porch door, and seeing the gray haze, the mist that coats the pines across the road. A small wind pushes at the screen door, makes it bang against the frame, gives her a rhythm she can count on: slap, pause, wind blow open, slap, pause, wind blow open, slap.

The phone will have rung while she was in the kitchen fixing this third cup of coffee, the one she planned to give to Stu but instead wanted herself. Rachel answers the phone before it can ring twice, picks it up and says a soft hello. After the phone call she remembers how Rose took forever to answer, to say her name, to begin speaking, to tell Rachel. Yes she was coming, don't worry, and how was she anyway, how did she feel?

Before it rings, she will know it is Rose.

Before it rings, she will see a spider fall from her hair.

She jerks the coffee from her to prevent the spider from landing there.

Before the phone call, but after the spider appears, Stu comes into the kitchen with a whistle, wanting to know how it was that she got up before him. They are the first ones awake. His shirt is misbuttoned and they are both nervous, knowing what day this is. Stu places his palm in the open space of his shirt above his breast and moves his hand around to his neck and rotates his head and says he must have slept funny because he feels all stiff. Rachel points to the spider. Stu picks it up by a leg, opens the back door, and tosses it out into the yard. They keep missing the chance to kiss. Stu moves toward his coffee cup at the moment Rachel reaches for him and he pops his elbow into her cheek in this accidental mismanagement of space. Her cry, his apology, this series of moves all make them laugh, make them seize upon one another finally.

The first in a long series of embraces—so starts a day of embraces between the two of them. At the end of this day their embraces will be the married kind and she wonders if they will be different. This man with graying hair, and a misbuttoned shirt, who is almost twice her age, he'll be her husband. He'll look out for her and be a father to her baby and she'll be his wife. His wife, her husband. These words are hard to say. I'm Stu's wife, she practices. Stu's wife. Her husband.

At the end of this embrace, Stu holds his hand at the back of Rachel's head and weaves his fingers into her hair. He calls this hair his gold, his perfumed gold, the heavenly money in a dowry neither of them may spend. She tells him to stop being silly, and pulls away from him, and from the stirring she feels, too, the bursting in her stomach. It is the breaking up of the distance between them, as though it were a building being dismantled, or an ice floe, or a balloon deflating. A laugh pops out of her. She directs him to the tree where there is still a bough hanging that says, Wedding. After that, all the growth is green and new, and has to do with their future, their baby, their life after this Get Married Day. Even the thick Mother branch has fallen off in the night, and Stu props it now against the back door, to be taken out and thrown away.

Stu takes their wedding garland from the refrigerator, wraps it around him, around his neck and chest and holds the ends up with his arms so that they won't drag on the floor. He twirls, and the garland swings out around him, honeysuckle arms, and he spins through the swinging kitchen door, singing the wedding march.

The phone rings and it is Rose, calling to say she's coming.

Rose will cut sunflower stalks from the garden and bring them as her guests, as a bouquet, as five pecked faces at the end of long stalks with flapping green arms that Rose will hold out, as though they were her own, for other guests to shake whenever she is introduced.

Rachel will cry, at least twice. She'll be happy, too. She is marrying the man she loves.

Ethan will start drinking early, and hard, but he will not at any point seem drunk, or do anything inappropriate.

The room will fill, and hum.

Bees will appear around the wedding garland, collect pollen, make a buzzing curtain, and disappear.

The sun will emerge from behind thick clouds, cutting through like a wedge, like a knife, like a burnished mass of white, glowing yellow at the edges, and warm.

When she comes down the back stairs to the kitchen early that morning (before Stu is up, before the phone call, or the spider, or the bees), Rachel first greets the Wedding List Tree, which springs open another blossom in response, a pink paper flower growing from a bud. As she opens the refrigerator to check on the garland and the cake, the sweet smell of honeysuckle and icing greets her, explodes over her. She closes the door and the smell lingers. She opens the window over the sink and breathes offshore air: salt, marsh, loam—peaty smells that have dew and part of the night still in them. She leaves the window open while she goes to make coffee, and the moist, spring morning, humid, blows through the curtain, plays at her face in small gusts, has her thinking in quick instants, of kite-flying, high school track, and camping out.

She tries not to be nervous, but there she is, alone, still the only one up. For a moment, in a second's time, she wonders what would happen if she lost the baby—today. At this moment, she admits for the first time that she can't say the words *husband*, *wife*, *marriage*. She tries them on. This is my husband, she practices saying, her hand moving midair. I'm Stu's wife. She stands at the sink, looks out the window, makes the years move behind her back, makes the baby grow and get born and grow still more until he is three and Stu is thirty-eight and they're at the kitchen table behind her, talking about something, monsters maybe and whether or not they can live on dirt. And she wonders if three years from now she will be able to say the words, and what she will have given up to make them not seem so strange in her mouth. I'm Stu's wife, she practices. This is Stu Hodge, my husband.

These words make her tongue loll about in strange ways, like high school French. She walks to the pantry with these words, these awkward vowels, filling her mouth, and stands in that small dim space looking out the back door at the porch to see a crow walking tightrope across the empty clothesline. I'm Stu's wife, she says slowly. Then fast. I'mStu'swife. She can see her lips moving in front of her mouth. The line sways as the bird steps sideways, then trots forward, then alights with a surprised call. As she says these three words, she watches her lips move below her eyes and she giggles, feeling sillier, wanting at this moment to rush outside, take off her clothes, be a bird, fly.

But she tells herself not to do these things, just as she tells herself each winter not to fall into fresh snow, not to lie down in it, not to make angels. This is her mother in her, she thinks, and her mother's mother and the mother before that, all those mothers telling daughters what is ladylike, and not.

Her mother will be there, at the wedding.

Her mother will leave, and Rachel will not tell her about how she, Rachel, will be a mother.

Stu is her family now. She is going to be Stu's wife.

Rachel still finds it hard to believe she will be a mother. Before she came downstairs, she was upstairs in the bathroom, naked, measuring her belly. She keeps the tape hidden in the cabinet under the sink, and every morning now she measures her belly to see if it has grown, to see how much the baby has grown. She's been keeping track. In the past month alone her stomach has gained three inches, and she swears, feeling it each morning, that she can sense something hard beginning to form there, even though she knows from the books Stu's bought that her baby is still only a few inches long. While she measures, she talks to it as though it were a plant, or a pet, urging it to grow. This morning, she reminds her baby that this is the day she and Stu will be married. That's one promise to you I've kept, she says. Not bad, not bad, she thinks, considering her odds up to now.

A second later, she slams hard against the promises she'll break. They make her curl over. They make her know she cannot protect this child, her baby.

In this moment, Rachel yearns to project her already projected self, from the wedding day to come to the future expanse of motherhood. She wishes she could imagine all the promises she won't keep. The emptiness terrifies her; she is not prepared. The tape slips from her waist, drops to the floor. She shivers, leans over, feels her naked breasts touch her stomach. She stares at the map-of-the-world shower curtain in front of her as though seeing it for the first time, and she notices that Taiwan is shaped like the patch of hair below Stu's belly button. She lets herself wonder about the various possible shapes of the baby growing inside her, even though she knows it will scare her even more. Lately, in her dreams the baby appears to her like worms and lizards— greenish-brown things with only heads and tails. She maps a trail across the shower curtain of the places she has always wanted to see, other continents, big triangular countries where the people eat odd food with their hands. Rachel wants to travel to these places, colored green and blue and yellow on the shower curtain, and as her eyes hop from one bright mass to another, she feels the hard thing growing in her, and she presses on it until it hurts, holding in her breath, too, until she can feel her cheeks expand and her chest constrict.

She puts her head between her legs and keeps it there until the blood rushes to the top of her skull and makes the place behind her eyes pound.

She does not feel well. Her stomach lets go with a long explosion, loud.

Rose will call and come and bring five sunflower friends and hold their green palms out for Stu to shake and Ethan will appear, suddenly sober, and he'll ask them all to give him an object to sacrifice. Something you're attached to, he says, something you have to give up to begin the slow and steady process of clearing your lives of unnecessary debris. This is how Ethan talks. He gives up his totem, makes Rose hand over her sunflowers, Stu a favorite flannel shirt, and Rachel—what will she abandon? There is nothing. She has nothing to toss into the bonfire Ethan has made on the beach. They try to make her think of something, make her go through the contents of her life. She laughs and shows her dimple and shrugs at the pile of objects in front of her that they have her pull out—an old set of jacks, a book of fairy tales, postcards from the places she's passed through, an ugly gray cowboy hat with a cigarette burn on the brim—and she tells them that they can take their pick but that any one of those things, or none of them, could easily go into the fire as far as she is concerned.

She is not attached, and yet this day will make her attached.

She'll stand on the porch and watch them on the beach, her new odd family, burning the things that attach them to the world. She'll walk across the chilly sand to join up with Stu and Ethan and Rose, her second march of the day.

They could be a family.

She and Stu would stand among borrowed folding chairs in secondhand clothes to face the justice of the peace from another county and exchange vows, and admit their middle names to each other for the first and last time.

Strangers would kiss her, the bride, and men would slap Stu on the back, and they'd walk off the porch, under the honeysuckle banner and past the bees, and there would be rice tossed over their heads.

Rachel can't imagine this. She can go all the way backward, but she can't get past the point when she and Stu would stand next to each other and *get married*. It is inconceivable to her.

Before she sits naked on the toilet to measure her belly, before she rolls those strange foreign words around in her mouth and laughs and imagines flight, before any of this wedding day can begin, Rachel lies beside Stu and tries to project herself past this moment. She will get out of this bed and start this day that will end in her marriage.

19

She will marry the man lying next to her.

She carries his child inside her. It is growing, getting harder, filling up the space that those small burstings create. It pushes her out, toward Stu, and it anchors her with its weight.

She is attached.

Stu is her family now.

Rachel feels Stu's warmth, his bulk beside her, filling the space next to her with breadth and mass. When she opens her eyes, the day will begin; all these simple images will make themselves real, or be interrupted by other moments beyond her imagination. Stu moves beside her, turning over and taking the blanket with him. This punctuated by a long breath, a sigh, that ends in a cough.

In the growing day, Rachel hears a bird, a fog horn, the sea. It is still so early and so quiet. So empty, just now. ❀

What promises have you already made to this baby-to-be? What promises have you already broken or anticipate breaking? Describe a scene you imagine in the future with your baby. What scene or aspect of mothering do you find difficult to imagine?

Date _____

Now That I Am Forever with Child

Audre Lorde

*H*ow the days went
while you were blooming within me
I remember each upon each—
the swelling changed planes of my body
and how you first fluttered, then jumped
and I thought it was my heart.

How the days wound down
and the turning of winter
I recall, with you growing heavy
against the wind. I thought
now her hands
are formed, and her hair
has started to curl
now her teeth are done
now she sneezes.
Then the seed opened
I bore you one morning just before spring
My head rang like a fiery piston
my legs were towers between which
A new world was passing.

Since then
I can only distinguish
one thread within running hours
You, flowing through selves
toward You.

In the first trimester when it isn't certain if the pregnancy will hold, we celebrated how this presence had already altered our lives and identities forever. Right now, how are you already "forever with child"?

Date _____

The Real Deal:
One Woman's Pregnancy Journal

Kimberley Evans Rudd

Some women have mixed feelings when they discover they're pregnant. But at age twenty-eight, working full-time with good medical benefits and in a good three-year-old marriage to a great man, I was ready. And as the little pink "positive" on my home pregnancy test proved, I was able.

So when I began my pregnancy journey in August 1995, I had a pretty positive and realistic attitude about the aches and pains and emotional ups and downs I would experience, or so I thought. Two years earlier I had been pregnant for fifteen weeks before I miscarried, so I figured I knew what pregnancy was about. Hah! What I didn't know could fill a book. This journal, offered in the interest of sisterly sharing, is a little of what I learned along the way. I guess you could call it "One Woman's Tale of How She Survived Pregnancy and Lived to Love Her Babies."

Month One

I've never been much of a record keeper when it comes to tracking my periods, so it has taken me a week or so to notice that I'm late. Recently my husband, David, and I took our trip of a lifetime, a roadie from Chicago to the Grand Canyon and Las Vegas. Today, six weeks and one missing-in-action period later, I rely on a home pregnancy test and a doctor's gestation wheel to deduct that it was during our vacation that The Deed was done. We're pregnant! And to think we complained about some of the cheap hotels on the road. I guess those lumpy beds aren't so bad after all!

Month Two

You know the singsongy kid's chant: "First comes love, then comes marriage, then comes a baby in a baby carriage"? Well, I'd like to insert before the last line, "then comes a whole bunch of doctor visits where you are pricked, prodded, and pumped, then comes baby in a baby carriage." At my first doctor's visit, I'm thinking I only have to prepare myself for having six vials of blood drawn. But that needling is nothing compared to the shock I get two minutes into my first ultrasound when the doctor speaks these immortal words: "You're pregnant with twins."

The moving picture of two hearts pumping is overwhelming. I can't believe my luck. Or fate. Can I handle two? Can we afford two? Exactly how big will I become? (I already weigh nearly 200 pounds, far too big for my five-foot-four-inch frame.) Somewhere between the doctor's office and the walk to meet my husband, the thought hits me: Maybe this is God's way of blessing my family with both a "new" baby and the one we'd lost.

Dave and I meet on a downtown corner at the height of lunchtime. People are walking by us quickly, on their way to take care of business. And I'm about to tell Dave that his life is going to change forever. Here he is thinking I'm just going to confirm the home pregnancy test. That alone would make his day. But I've got bigger news. "Dave, I was going to make up a story to play a trick on you, but I can't. I just have to tell you this straight out. Yes, we're pregnant and guess what? It's twins." I think the man actually staggers. He's stunned, I'm stunned, we're ecstatic. The next evening we get our parents together to tell them that their only children are pregnant with twins. We videotape their yahoo reaction. Life is great.

Month Three

Life sucks. Or rather, food sucks, throwing up sucks, going to work sucks. I'm not having a good month. I've lost fifteen pounds, can't keep food down, and am tired of driving to and from work with a plastic hurl bag at the ready. I had to celebrate my birthday clean and sober—no giddy toast with girls and our brandy alexanders. My only joy is that I'm enduring all this for the eventual treasure of having children.

We're taking lots of precautions. When I miscarried, the fetal tissue had an extra chromosome that would have caused severe defects, so now my doctor wants to do his best to ensure that these fetuses are genetically healthy. That's why I just went for a cvs (chorionic villus sampling) test, which checks the genetic makeup of the baby. It's a doozy. Using an ultrasound to guide him, the doctor stuck a long needle through my abdomen, uterus, and placenta. My bladder had to be full so that the ultrasound would be most effective. Because the doctor was pressing down extra hard on my belly and because they had to stick me twice—with about an hour between tries—I thought for sure I'd pee on someone before the afternoon was over. I didn't. We'll have to wait a week for the results, and we don't even want to think about what we'll do if they come back showing something is wrong.

By the end of this month, Dave and I are relieved to learn that both babies have a perfect twenty-three pairs of chromosomes. We also learn the genders, but have decided to tell only our parents. With all this good news and my moving out of the iffy first trimester, I finally tell coworkers that I'm pregnant. It feels good; it's amazing how people rally around the beginning of a new life.

Month Four

My oily, pimply first-trimester face gives way to what friends call my pregnant glow. My bloatedness starts to turn into a "showing." And my overall health gets thumbs-up from the doctor. Life looks up. Still, the physical and emotional changes are a trip. My hair is already rejecting a relaxer (I had heard that hormonal changes in later months sometimes cause this), so it's looking pretty rough. And I'm noticing that my scalp is flaking a lot, a problem I've never had before. I'm fairly irritable too, especially if my must-have evening naps are interrupted. And dry skin? Whoa! Is it ever. I'm now weighing 186 pounds, and surprise! I'm OK with that. Because what I used to hate—the roundness of my stomach—is now a source of joy.

Month Five

Ummm, oranges, Popsicles, hot sauce, Snickers bars. These are a few of my favorite things. But I have to watch carefully so as to avoid indigestion or gas—last night I was in the grocery store and found myself looking for an empty aisle to fart in. I used to control those suckers, but now they control me and are relentless. I hope this part of pregnancy passes, pardon the pun.

Oddly, my growing stomach makes me feel a little sexy. I wonder why. Meanwhile, anybody who asks to touch my stomach is welcome—I'm so amazed by its firmness, bigness, and enclosure of life that I understand how others could be, too. One coworker, deep into his African- and Native-American heritage, went so far as to perform a blessing on my stomach the other day, blowing incense around me and chanting calming words. Now that was a first. And it's confirmed: At week 18 I'm feeling real movements, not those silly "butterfly flutters" I'd read about.

Month Six

I no longer feel sexy—just big. But I also feel big movements. This is the most amazing part of my pregnancy. The babies are not these abstract beings anymore—they are moving, stretching, hiccuping people with personalities. Twin A is a rocker and a roller, rambunctious at night, often waking me up and certainly shoving the other twin around at times. Twin B has movements that are more fluid, less jerky. I think this one's going to be pensive. Sometimes I just sit around and think about who they will be, what they will look like, and what I'll look like after they are born.

Already I'm starting to swell in places other than my stomach: A ring was stuck on my finger for several days, and my feet are too big for all but two pairs of shoes. My waistline is about 41 inches, and the stretch pants that were too big in the waist and hips two months ago are now well stretched. Yesterday I got stuck in my car for a moment, trapped between the seat and the steering wheel. I must've looked like a circus attraction as I tried to get out. And my hair is just pitiful. I feel like making a button that says, "I'm not normally this tacky-looking and slow-moving—I'm just pregnant and tired."

Ok, enough of these put-downs, girl! I'm pregnant and just have to realize that emotionally and physically I'm just not my normal self. Crying spells, cursing frenzies, moody blues, and laughing fits—they are all a part of me for now. Even my hubby ain't looking so attractive to me; that old he-got-me-into-this-mess thing. But other men? I'm spottin' cuties left and right—at the very time that I don't want anybody looking at me!

Month Seven

I'm really beginning to fill out the maternity outfits my mother and aunt made for me, and I'm starting to feel pregnant in new ways. First of all, I am no longer sleeping with ease. Just as I was getting used to sleeping on my back, my increased weight and the abdominal pressure make even that position uncomfortable. The sleep deprivation leaves me cranky, especially when I'm awake while Dave sleeps soundly.

Second, I now have two hemorrhoids. Until this moment I've never paid much attention to TV commercials showing old people grimacing while holding up boxes of medicated cream or pads. Now I've got my own cream and a new inspiration to eat fibrous foods—I'm doing all I can to make sure I have easy bowel movements.

Next, contrary to popular belief, pregnancy does not relieve you of the need for sanitary napkins. I don't have a menstrual flow, of course, but I do have vaginal secretions caused by all the estrogen in my body. The estrogen is also causing me to develop more and bigger moles and pigment changes. Some women get the mask of pregnancy on their face; my darker skin is on my neckline.

Everybody's telling me that the glory months of the middle trimester are over and that I had just better get ready for the hard part of pregnancy now. The bigger my belly gets, the more inclined people are to dig out those horrific stories of tragic labors and deliveries. I think the hardest part of pregnancy is learning to tune that stuff out.

Month Eight

My fashion options are quite limited now. I wonder if my coworkers are mumbling to themselves, "Here she comes again in those black pants." I'm mixing and matching pieces so much, I feel as if I have on Garanimals. I miss wearing belts. The only one I've worn for months now is a thick elastic number to ease back strain. And it has been forever since I've worn high heels. My feet are so big that when I'm not at work, I wear my husband's sneakers. Finally, though, I've found pantyhose and tights that fit! Before, in maternity stores, I could only find one-size-fits-all hosiery—what a lie! My hips are as big as a twelve-year-old is tall; one size does not fit me!

I had a great doctor's visit today. I got to see the twins again, via my third ultrasound. The doctor checked the babies' sizes to make sure that they are sharing nutrients and that one baby isn't growing at the expense of the other. They are lying in a bunk-bed position, Twin A on top and Twin B on bottom. Now I know why I feel as though I'm getting kicked in the ribs. It looks as though the babies are beginning to turn and settle into a normal headfirst position and that I have a good chance of having a vaginal delivery.

Month Nine

I've stopped working. Twins are often born around week 36, so the doctor and Dave have pretty much confined me to the house. Rather than listen to the clock tick while waiting for the babies, I do stuff. I talk to my mother, who's visiting. I crochet the babies' hats (I'm bored before I finish the second one). I address announcement envelopes. Nothing keeps me from wondering, When, oh when, will my water break?

At the baby shower given by my girlfriends, we have a contest to guess my waistline. The answers range from the mid-forties to a high of eighty-six inches! Dag, do I look that big? I'm about forty-nine inches and proud of it. My size and the length of my pregnancy are signs of healthy babies. So are the results of my weekly NSTS (nonstress tests) that monitor the babies' heartbeats for consistency. Still, I can't help but have a few bad dreams about labor and delivery. I don't think I've ever prayed as much in my life as I have this month.

Month Ten

I wasn't supposed to make it this far! At week 38, I can hardly believe it. What happened to that "twins are born early" theory? Here I am, still carrying my 211 pounds to the doctor (twice a week) to get poked, prodded, and asked to pee into a cup. Even the parking-lot attendant is impatient: "Are you still pregnant?"

I know it has to end soon. My doctor hints at inducing labor shortly if the babies don't come on their own. A friend tells me to swig mineral oil and orange juice, which she claims is a midwife's way to bring labor. I do, and end up with a mild case of diarrhea, much to my hemorrhoids' pleasure. Others tell me to "walk those babies out" or watch a funny movie and "laugh them out." I do, and end up winded from the walking and broke from the movies.

At week 39, my dilation hasn't progressed well, so the doctor will induce labor. I wanted a traditional labor, one where your water breaks suddenly, you run through the house screaming at your family, then you zoom to the hospital, where you holler and grunt, then pop! out comes a baby. But now I want whatever it'll take to end this forever-long pregnancy and give me my babies. I am to report to the hospital on Tuesday at 7 P.M., the end of my fortieth week.

Epilogue

My labor began near midnight that Tuesday evening—assisted with IV drops of oxytocin, a drug that causes the uterus to contract. Soon I had the most incredible cramps ever and decided there was no sense being a martyr: "An epidural, please," I said. "Numb me. Make me woozy. Knock me out." Two hours later I still had no epidural pumping into my spine and realized I'd been too polite in my request. "Give me drugs!" I yelled. That time it worked. For nearly three hours the pain was manageable. Then the real fun began.

It was Wednesday morning, and I was told to push. To give me resistance, Dave held one leg and a young nurse held the other. Despite the fear that my pushes would send all three of us flying into a wall—I mean, my legs must've weighed more than that nurse—I pushed and moaned and delivered Twin B, Gregory, at about 9:30 A.M. Victoria, Twin A, was having a more difficult time, taking longer than the traditional twenty minutes or so to be born after the first baby. There was some talk of doing a cesarean section, but Victoria had a healthy heartbeat and I felt I could push more, so we labored. I didn't want to face healing from both a C-section and an episiotomy (a cut between the birth canal and anus to provide more passing room for the baby's head). Finally, Victoria made her entrance, some ninety minutes after her brother. Both babies were healthy and beautiful, a total of nearly fourteen pounds, and Dave and I were overwhelmed with joy.

Most amazing is that in spite of the discomfort of the next days—chills, headaches, cramps and contractions, pain from my episiotomy stitches, horrible fear of having a bowel movement, and sore, sore nipples from breast-feeding—I had done it. I had survived pregnancy and lived to love my babies. ❀

Fantasy and reality always differ. In what ways are your dream and real-life pregnancies different and the same? How might the differences coincide with your imagined and real-life experiences of motherhood?

Date _____

Early Morning Woman

Joy Harjo

early morning woman
rising   the sun
         the woman
bending and stretching
with the strength of the child
that moves
in her belly

early morning makes her
a woman that she is
the sun
is her beginning
it is the strength
that guides her child

early morning woman
she begins that way
        the sun
        the child
are the moving circle
beginning with the woman
in the early morning ❦

Make up a song or chant for you and your baby. In it, give yourself and your baby special names or epithets.

Date _____

Maternity

Amy Halloran

I've never liked to talk about clothes or appearances, the things that tend to dominate female conversations. But now that I'm pregnant we're on common ground. I finally feel camaraderie with women. I need to know the basics. I look mothers in the eye, as if to find the secrets of surviving labor and sleep deprivation. Was your mother worried when you told her you were pregnant? What did you do for clothes? How much help will I want when I get home from the hospital? I ask these questions to my neighbors. I live in a young mother's ghetto, a cheap quiet neighborhood with yards. These women are my peers, but until recently I didn't know them. They had kids and that scared me. Now I can hear about C-sections and home births and the fear and awe of a father-to-be. The doorbell rings and someone needs eggs for cookies and I get advice on which hospital I should use. Sure, I'm shocked when I look at pregnancy books and see what is happening inside of me, but I'm just as surprised, and in a better way, to find I've joined the club of women for keeps.

Not that the advice from other members is always welcome. When I wasn't even showing I began to be bombarded by stories from other mothers. I've decided there are two categories of tellers, those who listen while they tell their stories and those who don't. The latter are doomed to repeat and repel their audiences, and they attack at cocktail parties and yoga classes, wherever they find their pregnant prey. From their examples, I hope I am learning to listen.

"Wait till you get over morning sickness," said a sage drunk one Saturday. "The difference will be night and day."

"I know," I said, "I'm over it," but she told me again, as if I hadn't spoken.

"The difference will be night and day," she said again.

"I know, it is," I said again, louder in case I hadn't been heard.

"Night and day," she said, holding my arm for emphasis.

"I'll take your word for it," I said, trying to get away.

The following Tuesday, after yoga, a woman accosted me while I was tying my shoes. I had my head bent to the task as if it were very demanding. The teacher had suggested alternate poses for those of us who were pregnant. This was unnerving—the first time anyone had announced my status before strangers.

"Are you going to have a midwife?" the excited classmate asked. I tried to avoid the intensity of her eyes, but they were magnified by her glasses.

"I'm going to have an epidural, but I haven't decided whether to have an obstetrician or a midwife," I said. Midwives work in hospitals in my state, so it is possible to get the best of both worlds.

"But you have to transcend the pain!" she told me, getting her face too close to mine.

"I'm glad you did, but I have other things on my agenda," I told her. Even after my shoes were tied, this woman kept trying to convince me that I should give birth the way she had.

If I were a man, I could have turned these chats into challenges. As things are, I have to accept opinions instead of argue ideas. What, I wonder, separates the desperate lecturers from the rest? What can I do to avoid becoming like them, to keep from pouring my story into the nearest ear? Because I am sure I will have to tell it.

Usually I tell my story as it is happening, writing in a journal or mailing my feelings off in letters or postcards. But the me I know is changing. I am not Amy Anna Halloran, thirty-year-old writer. I am Amy Anna Halloran, mother-to-be, a title that's hard to hold. The first two months I was pregnant I was so frightened I didn't write anything at all, not having the perch of an identity to pontificate from.

I still don't have a picture of who I'm becoming. There's the terrifying prospect of becoming my mother, but I don't want to be her, because I want to stick with my art. She's a visual artist, and for years of my youth she pursued her sight. I remember a show she had of stuffed fabric busts. These soft people were called The Cocktail Party and hung by fish line at eye level. Eventually my mother stopped making art and began making things, crafty gifts for holidays. She remained creative but the vein she mined was thinner, in my opinion. Now she's turned my bedroom into a studio and she is constantly making prints—I'm thrilled, but I worry that I will leave my tracks too, until my kids are grown. I used to think she changed her goals because of her role in rearing us, but now, having experienced a certain amount of artistic discouragement myself, I see that lots of factors could have stemmed her enthusiasm.

Jack tells me not to worry, that I am too driven to give up what I want. I'm not so easily convinced. It wasn't hard for him to persuade my biology to sway my fate. My plumbing leaped at the offer of his needs. A week after we began to be together, I knew I would have his kids. None of this was articulated. How will I remind myself of my dreams?

I can only hope I stick to my guns, that I'll keep writing about the changes as my footing feels out quicksand. I must make myself find places where I can look down at myself like an owl, writing out wisdom as the umbrella of motherhood unfolds. ❦

Are you aware of any way your identity as a woman feels different now that you're pregnant (or pregnant again)? How is your relationship to other women changing? How do you respond to being given advice about pregnancy? Is this different from how you respond to advice in general? What words of advice would you secretly like to hear? If you could look down on yourself "like an owl," what would you see?

Date _____

Baby Pictures

Molly Giles

The light's right, bright as foil, a long silver sheet rolling in through the east kitchen window. I take one look and race back to the bedroom. "Mama?" Wynn calls as I pound past his door. "Mama? It's up time?"

"One second," I tell him. I find the camera where I left it, on top of the laundry. I snatch at it fast and race back to the kitchen. The light is still there, and everything blazes: the toaster, the step stool, the pears set to ripen on the sill. The dishes Robert left piled in the sink are the loveliest things I've ever seen in my life. I clamp the camera to my eye and hold my breath. The soiled plates, crushed napkins, and empty wineglasses burst into focus, each edge as sharp as if carved from a mirror. I lean forward, add Wynn's battered cup, subtract one gutted white candle, lean back, smile. It's going to be good. I steady the camera, touch the shutter—and just as I do, the back door flies open and Leslie Carney's shadow leaps over my shoulder to darken the drainboard. I turn with both hands raised. "Don't shoot me," Leslie giggles.

"Don't tempt me," I warn her. She's gleaming with sweat from her morning run, her face flushed, her hair stuck to her forehead.

"I knocked," she says. "You just didn't hear me. I had to come over. I've got the best news. You won't believe it."

What I won't believe, I think, as I lower the camera, is how little it takes to lose a good shot. I sigh at the sink of soiled dishes—ordinary plates in ordinary daylight—and set the camera down. Leslie pulls a yellow leaf from her sweatshirt pocket, hands it to me, and grins at my bathrobe. It's a long red Chinese robe with a torn hem and a grass stain on the knee; it was made in Paris and lined in silk, and despite Leslie's grin I can tell she admires it. Leslie is a jeweler; she too works at home, and she would give anything, I know, to have a robe of rich red silk to work in. I wear this robe for that—for making my pictures—and because I am pregnant again and need clothes that are loose.

"I'd like champagne," Leslie says, "but it's eight in the morning so I'll settle for tea. What kind do you have? Anything with rose hips is fine. I like rose hips when I've got cramps and oh man do I have cramps. I've got my period. My wonderful period. Two weeks late but I've got my period."

"That's your news?"

"That's part of my news."

"Leslie's here," Wynn sings from the bedroom. "Up time, Mama. Breakfast for Wynn time."

"I mean, I don't want to sound tactless," Leslie says, watching me put a pot of water on to boil for tea, "but if I were pregnant again right now I would kill myself. If I had to start over and do what you do all day, I'd never have time for myself." She follows me down the hall to Wynn's room, her voice a light hiss at my heels.

Wynn has taken the pillowcase off his pillow and put it over his head. Since he is wearing nothing else, the effect is predictable, and Leslie, whose own children are ten and twelve and girls besides, stares at him sorrowfully and says, "See. I just couldn't take it." I scoop Wynn's damp pajamas and diapers from under the mattress where he has stuffed them, toss them toward the hamper, grab jeans and shirt from half-opened drawers, and carry him, kicking and singing, masked and naked, back into the kitchen.

"No bath?" he asks from beneath the pillowcase. "No bath today?"

"Later," I tell him. "He hates to have his hair washed," I explain to Leslie.

"They all do," Leslie says. I let it pass. Leslie is my age but acts like she's older. She's been married longer and had children earlier and seems to have always known what she wanted to do with her life. I feel as if I'm just beginning to find out. I started taking pictures five years ago—about the same time I met Robert—and I had my first, and last, exhibit the month before Wynn was born. It's hard, Leslie has told me, to handle marriage and children and career—hard, but not impossible. Leslie herself has lived in the same house with the same man for fourteen years, and she has worked on her jewelry steadily through pregnancies, breast-feedings, childhood illnesses, Scout troops, and orthodontists' appointments. If she can do it, I tell myself, so can I. I lift the pillowcase off Wynn's head and contemplate his rosy face.

"He threw up last night," I explain to Leslie. "In his crib. I didn't give him a full bath then because it was late and the tub was full of my trays and equipment."

"You need your own darkroom," Leslie says, shaking her head. "I've told you and told you . . ."

"He hasn't thrown up since," I interrupt. "I hope it's not flu."

"Lara used to throw up all the time when she was two," Leslie says. "It's their digestive systems. They aren't developed yet."

"Digestive systems," I repeat, impressed. Wynn, bouncing, singing, lets me dress him, then slips off my knees, runs into the living room, turns on the TV, and plumps down to a babble of cartoons. I am aware of Leslie's disapproval (she does not own a TV) and I feel that disapproval deepen as she watches me wander around the kitchen fixing Wynn's breakfast. The dry cereal, I realize, has too much sugar, the milk is not nonfat, the juice is not fresh-squeezed. Leslie contents herself with a brief sigh and starts to touch her toes. I carry Wynn's breakfast in to him, set it down, and kiss him softly on top of his head. His hair smells foul and as soon as Leslie leaves I'll start his bath. I dread it already. He'll fight. He'll hit me and scream. I'll scream and hit back. We'll both be drenched with bath water, struggling, slipping, cursing, he on his knees in the water, me on my knees on the tiles, both of us shouting "Stop it!", both of us in tears, neighbors phoning police, an ax splitting the door, sirens, trained dogs, a reporter calling Robert at the office.

Leslie is doing leg lunges when I come back in, her short solid body posed like an archer's in the doorway. "She's not like your other friends," Robert said when he met her. "She isn't crazy and she isn't pretty." I was surprised that Robert, usually so astute, could not see Leslie's beauty. Perhaps he's never noticed her eyes. They are small and half-hidden under the thick blond bangs she forgets to clip back, but they are beautiful eyes, shy, quick, and as luminous as the moonstones she works with. She works with ebony, ivory, and opals too. She designs bracelets and breastplates—big, heavy pieces—Amazon armor. She told me once, without smiling, that she was developing a personal mythology, based on her study of the goddess Artemis. I answered, unsmiling, that I knew what she meant. My goddess has neither name nor mythology, but I wait on her too, and watch for her blazing. Leslie straightens now and pats her flat stomach.

"You know what I'd be doing today if I hadn't gotten my period?" she asks. "I'd be at the clinic, waiting in line for an abortion. Carney would be in line behind me, with a gun at my back. You know how he is. The last thing he wants is a baby right now." Leslie assumes I know her husband better than I do, but in fact I've only met him once. Carney is a contractor who came to our house, alone, to talk about building a darkroom for me. I remember a slight, soft-spoken man in a baseball cap. There was nothing distinctive about him, and if I were to pass him on the street without his cap I would not be sure enough to say hello. Sometimes Leslie wears his cap when she rides her bike, but I always know Leslie, in all her disguises. I recognize her in her blue jeans, in her sweat suit, in the long lace dress she wears to the art fairs. I recognize her at the market, in the schoolyard, in front of the post office. We meet, I sometimes think, like spies; we hide behind our grocery bags the way spies hide behind newspapers. We stand in broad daylight and exchange secrets. We know all the passwords. Our password is "He."

"He," Leslie says now, "already made me have one abortion. Best thing he ever made me do, too." She takes the cup of tea I pour her and sits down at the table. "So," she says. "You've traveled all over. What's a good place to stay in New York?"

"New York? Who's going to New York?"

She grins. "Remember that craft show I applied for? Well, they took me. I got the letter yesterday. They liked the slides I sent—especially the series of winged headbands. They said my work was just what they were looking for. Man! Can you believe it?"

"Yes!"

We are shrieking and laughing across the table. "I'm so excited," Leslie cries. She claps her hands over her eyes. "But what do you think I should do?"

"Do? What do you mean? You should go."

"What if Carney won't let me?"

"Won't *let* you?"

"What if he tries to stop me?"

I laugh again. Leslie does not. Pouring my own tea, I say, "How can he stop you?"

"He broke my arm once."

I look up, shocked. Leslie shrugs. "I don't think he meant to. Some guy was coming on to me, once, at an opening; Carney thought I was flirting or something. He's kind of insecure lately. So he's not going to like the idea of me flying off for a week in New York."

"You mean you haven't told him yet?"

"I've been thinking I may never tell him. Until the night before I leave." She drops her eyes, stirs her tea. Wynn hollers, "More toast," and as I get up to make it I say, "You could take Carney with you."

"I can't afford his ticket. As it is, I'm going to have to use money he doesn't even know about. This friend of mine—this lawyer I met at the tennis courts—he helped me set up a special account. In my maiden name. Carney can't touch it."

I'm thinking what I'd give for a week with Robert in New York, but I don't say that. One of the best years of my life was spent with Robert in New York; we were starting out and everything was free and easy between us. We were determined to be different from other couples we knew—we were going to be kinder and smarter and more successful. We were never going to fight and we were going to share everything—dreams and responsibilities—equally. I block the breadboard so Leslie can't see me putting marmalade on Wynn's toast, and then I carry it in to him. When I come back to the kitchen I see that Leslie is leafing through a book of Imogen Cunningham's photographs on the table.

"What's your favorite?" she asks me.

"Favorite? That's hard. Maybe this one . . ." I open the book and point to a picture of an unmade bed, all soft folds and shadows. "I love this one. When Cunningham's children were little she did what I'm trying to do now—that is, she took pictures of things around the house and garden. Some of her best work was done when she was a housewife." I smooth my bathrobe over my belly, feeling the baby move, as I stare down at the picture. "It can be done," I say. I follow Leslie's speculative look toward the dishes in the sink, and laugh. "Those," I dismiss them, "those are Robert's. It was Robert's night last night. He was supposed to wash up but he forgot."

"Men don't do a damn thing," Leslie says.

I take a deep breath. "He," I say, "was supposed to watch Wynn and do the dishes last night so I could go to a lecture at the college. When I came home I found Wynn asleep in his crib with vomit on his blanket. Robert hadn't even undressed him. His shoes were still on."

Leslie shakes her head. We have finished our tea, but I don't make more. Thinking of Robert's laziness has made me lazy. Thinking of Robert's selfishness has made me want to withhold. I'm remembering how Robert tricked me into making love to him last night when I came home; that's what I cannot forgive—that he fooled me into all the old exhilaration, then let me pad by myself into our child's room, stretching, smiling in wifely content, to discover there the sort of man I'd married. I was angry last night and I'm angry today. Anger feels almost natural now, to me and to Robert too; we take it for granted, accept it as an everday mood. We no longer think of ourselves as a couple set apart. "His accounts . . ." I explain. "He said he had to work on his accounts and since I had 'so much free time' today . . ."

"Free time," Leslie repeats. She laughs. "The only time I feel free," she says, "is when I'm alone." Her words seem to surprise her, for she bends to tie her shoelace. I notice her left hand is bare. She told me once she had never liked her wedding ring; Carney had picked it out for her. "And you know Carney's taste." She straightens, drums her fingers on her knees, and says, "Men are such babies."

Wynn, at the sound of the word *babies*, comes running in and climbs on my lap. He sticks his tongue between his teeth and gets an absorbed, stupid look on his face as he starts to pull the front of my bathrobe open. "Don't do that," I warn him.

"Want to," Wynn says.

"No."

"*Want* to."

"It's hard when they're little," Leslie says. "You'll have more freedom next year." She turns to Wynn. "You be nice to your mother."

Wynn says, "No! *You* be nice!" He is about to say more when he hears the music of a favorite commercial. He gives me a brilliant smile, slips off my lap, and runs back to the television.

"Of course next year," Leslie continues, "you'll have the new one." She stands. "I've got to get going. Finish my run. I do twenty-five miles a week now. It's really amazing how strong I've grown." For a second I'm afraid she is going to make me feel one of her muscles, but her eyes are on the floor and her face looks sad. "I feel better than I ever have in my life," she says, "and the better I feel and the stronger I feel, the more restless I get. I can't explain it. I just feel . . . restless."

I know she is talking about sex. I am silent.

She sits down again, jiggles her knees up and down, and says, "The other night Carney and I were fooling around on the couch and I wrestled him down to the floor. You should have seen his face. Nothing like that had ever happened to him before in his life. He was so surprised. But he liked it too. Men like strong women. Just so long as they know they're still stronger." She throws me a knowing woman-to-woman smile that fades very fast. "When Carney and I were first married I couldn't drive a car. I couldn't balance a checkbook. I had to ask him for every cent before I went to the store. Now I do it all. I pay the bills and fix the car and put in the garden and he's just, you know, the same old Carney. Losing his hair. Getting a paunch. I feel sorry for him in a way. But I can't stop growing. I can't go backward. I have to go forward. What else is there?"

She is looking at me, expecting an answer. "Well . . ." I begin. I don't know how to finish. There is the second in between backward and forward that sometimes blazes and can sometimes be captured. But I can't explain that.

"It's not fair," she says flatly. "Someone's always losing. You can't gain something without someone else losing." She picks the yellow leaf off the table, pulls it apart. "The other day," she says, "I was talking to this guy, this lawyer, and he was telling me about a trail ride you can take, up into the Sierras, you rent your own horse, and I thought, Oh man, wouldn't I love to get away. Just get up and go, all by myself."

We are both silent. We are both imagining the Sierras, the high, dry sunlit air, the buzzing of bees, the flight of an eagle, the scent of sugar pine and smoke. I will take my camera, I think, and a knapsack of film. I will spend one day on clouds, one day on reflections, one day on . . . "Mama," Wynn sighs. He stands before me, aims, throws a toy car at my foot. It strikes and burns my ankle. "Thanks a lot," I tell him. He ducks his chin down. I can tell he is sorry. He doesn't like having Leslie here so early. He likes me to himself in the mornings. I like me to myself in the mornings too. "I want to get away," I say. There's a twitch to my voice—the anger that's become so familiar. "I want to get away and finish my portfolio. Do you know what's in my portfolio?"

Leslie shakes her head.

"Baby pictures," I say.

We both laugh. I think of my pictures: Wynn an hour old, a day old, a month old, a year . . . Wynn with Robert in the garden, at the beach, his arms around Robert's neck as Robert studies his accounts at the table . . . Wynn in a basket, a backpack, a walker, on foot . . . baby pictures. And although the baby changes in each one, turns into someone new who turns into someone else again, although the stately infant in lace becomes the radiant, skinny-legged shouter on the trike, although nothing has been lost or gained that I haven't caught, or tried to catch, at the instant of passing, although I have done my best, baby pictures they are, and remain. Leslie is right to treat me as someone younger, someone who still has a great deal to learn.

"Your time will come," Leslie promises. "Just hang on in. And oh, by the way, I have those earrings you wanted me to make for your mother-in-law. They're good. She'll like them."

"How much will you let me have them for?" I know Leslie's work is expensive, but she's already said she will give me a break.

"Money?" she says. "Let's see. I hadn't thought about money. You took those slides for me . . . let's say eighty."

"Dollars?"

"They'd sell for twice that at any gallery."

Too much, I think. Leslie and her husband both ask too much. Carney wanted a fortune to build the darkroom. Robert shook his head when I gave him the price. "You'll have to wait a little longer," Robert told me. But can I wait a little longer? I haven't sold a photo in over six months. At night I wake up wide-eyed, frightened. I listen to Robert breathing beside me; I get up and check on Wynn in his crib. I walk back and forth through the house in my bathrobe. I should take pictures then, in the dark; I should start a new series on insomniac housewives. Ghostly refrigerators, moonlight on mirrors, a bag of onions beginning to sprout. Leslie has told me she used to wake up too; she used the time to research Artemis.

She is explaining that gemstones are expensive as she clears off the teapot, rinses it, and sets it on the counter to dry. She tells me she uses only the finest materials. She tells me she has high standards and always manages to meet them. I know this. I approve. The little rabbit tails on her tennis socks flick as she paces around my kitchen. If I'm not interested in quality . . . if I want cheap stuff . . . "Leslie," I sigh. She subsides.

"I just don't want you to think I'm ripping you off," she mutters. "If you don't want to take them, someone else will."

"Let me think about it," I say. But I'm thinking that eighty dollars will make a good start toward building a darkroom. I walk Leslie to the door and watch her drop into her leg lunge again. The sun is strong as bleach now, stripping her hair, making her face, as she lifts it, shiny and tired. "I shouldn't have had that tea," she says. "It's going to slow me down. But thanks anyway." She turns, pauses, grins over her shoulder. "Where did you find that bathrobe again?"

"Paris," I tell her. "My first gift from Robert."

She groans and waves and I wave too as she jogs from sight. Then I close the door and look around the kitchen. I have to clean. I have to cook. I have to shop. I have to dress. I have to make one beautiful picture and then another and then a portfolio of beautiful pictures. But all I do is stand by the kitchen sink, eating crusts of toast off Wynn's breakfast plate, staring at the leaves falling onto the patio. I am remembering the last time I went to Leslie's house. We sat on the floor of her studio, surrounded by tools neatly nested in marked boxes, sunshine pouring in on everything, alchemizing even the smell of burnt metals into an essence airy, pure; we drank wine with our sandwiches and laughed because we were so lucky, because we had it all, home and husbands and children and good health and our own good work to do too. I turn from the sink. Wynn has been watching from the doorway. A shaft of mid-morning sun falls on his hair.

"Is it later yet?" he asks, and I know at once he means bath, is it time for the bath, time for our struggle.

"Not yet, my love."

"I don't like later."

"I don't like it either. I like now."

"What's now?"

"This."

I reach up, lift the camera off the top of the refrigerator where I left it, uncap the lens, and focus on Wynn. I catch him as he turns, hair filthy and on fire in the sunlight, already shouting, half gone, in flight. ❦

How have you been affected by remembrances and anticipation in your life? Has pregnancy changed or enhanced how you deal with past, present, and future, or how you hope to teach your baby to do it?

Date _____

My Baby Has No Name Yet

Kim Nam Jo *(translated by Ko Won)*

My baby has no name yet;
like a new-born chick or a puppy
my baby is not named yet.

What numberless texts I examined
at dawn and night and evening over again!
But not one character did I find
which is as lovely as the child.

Starry field of the sky,
or heap of pearls in the depth.
Where can the name be found, how can I?

My baby has no name yet;
like an unnamed bluebird or white flowers
from the farthest land for the first,
I have no name for this baby of ours. ✤

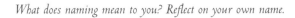

What does naming mean to you? Reflect on your own name.

Date _____

Seen and Not Seen

Anna Purves

You are pregnant and proceeding with it. You held off for three years, then tried and tried for another long year—of course you are proceeding with it. It is not as if you have any other way to go about doing this, you are a human, not a frog or a chicken. But your assaulted condition does not seem to have anything to do with a baby.

You are not so ridiculous as to think the process of dot to person would be a picnic, but the bare fact is that you are more ill than you have ever been in your life. It is worse than flu, shellfish poisoning, being dumped by your most in-love-with boyfriend. Ginger tea, raspberry tea, mint tea, Vitamin B shots, and crackers do nothing, absolutely nothing. The misery never stops except for an hour or so after midnight. Nobody is terribly concerned. They save their concern for medical emergencies, interesting ones that require bed rest and give rise to dramatic anecdotes. Instead of getting to be "interesting," you go onto your hands and knees and pant behind closed doors every day at work because the nausea gets worse when you sit upright for more than an hour. Nobody is concerned, because this is common enough to be customary and anyway, the embryo isn't affected.

You increase the number of times a day you throw up and how long you're at it. You lose it more than anyone you know has ever heard of, vomiting six or seven times a day, even water and crackers, especially water and crackers, and now you are on bed rest because your blood pressure is too low to let you stand up. You lose twenty pounds by the fourth month. Nobody is worried. You cannot bear to be kissed or touched. Reading or watching TV gives you painful vertigo. This is the longest trip you could ever imagine and you are on your own, kiddo.

When you are admitted for the second time to the emergency room for dehydration, they decide to keep you a little longer than overnight. You think this is good because they'll finally care about you too, not just the thing they call the fetus. However, it turns out they still won't give you Compazine, not even a little bit, but they are going to take a picture in case there's anything unusual going on.

You know what this means. Everyone talks about this relatively new technical ability; millions of expectant mothers have these pictures taken. The technician on duty is very kind and swivels the monitor exactly at your eye level so you don't have to raise your head and start heaving, again. On the screen appears a head, a curved spine, and two splayed hands that look like they are clapping. Underneath the hands are the tucked up legs and a beating heart. It is definitely a baby in there and it is fine. The technician makes a print of the picture for you to keep. He has no idea what he has done. He has allowed you, through little fault of his own, really, to see the invisible. Nine months is a short time after the fact; an endless existence during. But you've seen the baby. You can make it now. You think of that psalm where they say, "My frame was not hidden from you [God] when I was being made in secret, intricately woven in the depths of the earth." Even then everyone wanted to know what they couldn't know. And now you and the technician can see the things that God sees all the time.

Every morning on the instant you wake up, you see a huge, blown-up version of the baby in your mind's eye. You remain absolutely still, so as not to ignite the heaving mechanism, and dwell instead on the waving hands, the shimmering dark and light image that flickers like a movie from the 1920s.

The week after you return from the hospital, you have more than a vision. You have a visitation. The baby is floating in front of you in the early morning light. Your husband is shaving in the bathroom, unaware of this hallucinatory event. The baby, still encased in his black-and-white TV image, calls you over to him and you go, so fast you feel like you are on board a rocket ship. You traverse all the Himalayas and every other geographic barrier known to humankind, without even sitting up on the pillows. Immediately after you cross over, you are suddenly filled with terrible fear: a previous commitment seems to have just been dismissed. Heart and soul to one must be nominal for another; it cannot be possible to be all for more than one other person. The wind of pure panic is in your ears. After all, you are a person who values her values and her given word as though wrought of gold and diamonds. You summon your husband because a terrible transgression has just occurred that requires equally instant confession. You announce that you have gone over to the baby and you have never known such love. You love this uterine being more than him, you tell him. You have split time itself in half: ten years for him that just this minute ended and utter, eternal fealty for the one that hasn't even arrived. You sit at the fulcrum of past and future, waiting for the present to be ashes at your feet. There is no firestorm. Your husband doesn't look even mildly perturbed. He tells you, "Of course you love the baby more. You are supposed to. *Nobody* can compete with a baby." He goes off whistling and shaving. When you were preparing for your wedding some years ago, you felt the tectonic plates of the continent shift and readjust themselves underneath your feet. But those were only tremors; the advent of the absolute relationship is the real shakeup.

The sun is fully risen now. You adjust the bandage on your forearm which holds the rehydration IV in place and get up, automatically careful to neither see nor smell any kind of food, and attend to your affairs. You have connected with someone an ocean away whose existence thus far you could only assume by inference, just like the prophets and the Hebrew kings inferred three, four thousand years ago. Because of victory in battle and plagues of locusts they said God was manifest. Because of changes in blood, urine, and mood they tell you that you will have a child. You always did things just in case there really was a God, but you couldn't believe without seeing. Signs weren't enough, you needed the thing itself.

When the child passes through the gate five long months later, you are filled with regulation amazement and happiness. But you knew him when he was a secret, you saw him. And with no mouth and no eye he called you.

How has the being inside you called to you? How have you called back? What are you doing "just in case" for the sake of this being? What are the difficult or challenging emotions you are coping with regarding sharing your body with this being? When did you find yourself hopelessly in love or totally committed to him or her?

Date _____

Evie

Chelo Diaz-Ludden

*S*he dozed, cocooned in the blanket with only a foot sticking out into the cool quiet morning air. As she rolled over, she cupped her hand on the warm roundness of her belly, dreaming of the primal life inside, curling and stretching, its paleness barely perceptible in the dark watery world.

From the nightstand the alarm began buzzing . . . buzzing . . . buzzing. She gently jabbed him in the back. "It's 7 o'clock." He stood up and she felt the mattress lift under her. As he lumbered toward the bathroom, she glimpsed the white roundness of his buttocks, the edges blurred by a light covering of hair. She stretched and sprawled sideways, listening sleepily to the splash of his urine in the toilet, then the downpour of the shower.

The stillness of the bedroom was broken with his routine morning noises, the quiet sliding of the closet door, the muted clicking of the hangers when he groped for his robe hung on a hook in the back. As she listened to the muffled padding of his feet hitting the carpet down the hall, a thought slipped into her somnolent mind; she hadn't seen his face, hadn't fully opened her eyes, she had only heard him move around the room. He could be a stranger, any man, stirring in the shadows of her bedroom.

Evie needed to see his face. She felt gullible, tricked by her own thoughts, but threw on an oversized T-shirt, covering the goose bumps on her skin, and strode out to the kitchen. He stood at the sink filling the coffee pot, and scratching his heel with his long bare toes. John turned and smiled, his wet hair still showed teeth marks from the comb.

"How's my little *mamacita* this morning?"

"Fine," she murmured, his familiar voice soothing the goose bumps on her skin.

"No more morning sickness?" She felt his warm breath on the nape of her neck as his hands slid up under the front of her T-shirt. "They're getting big."

"I feel like a cow."

"Let's see if we can milk them."

"You'll be late for work." She stepped back.

His lips tightened. "Yeah, I'll be late for work, you're going to puke." He turned away from her. "What's wrong with you lately? Fucking is for more than making babies you know."

"John . . . don't be an ass. I'm going back to bed." She turned and fled down the hall.

"You don't even kiss me anymore," he shouted after her.

Evie crawled into the sheets and covered her head with the quilt as she listened to him noisily open and slam drawers, swear as he searched for a matching pair of socks, and finally stomp through the living room and kick the front door closed.

He was wrong, right in a way, but wrong. Something in her had changed, her skin still responded to his touch, but her mind revolted. She blamed the fat that padded her everywhere; overnight it had floated to the surface and jelled. She was surprised that he didn't see it, wasn't repulsed by it.

An hour later, Evie got up and made herself a cup of coffee, half strength because though caffeine wasn't good for the baby, she was lost without it. She took out her small notebook to make a list of things to do that day, but after doodling a few minutes ripped it out and threw it away.

As she drove toward the ocean, the bright sun and blue sky of San Marcos gradually dimmed. The change satisfied her and she began to look forward to indulging in a gloomy day. John had been so wrapped up in her motherhood from the beginning. He'd straightened and started that fertile strut of males she found both irritating and endearing. His hands began measuring the growing fullness of her breasts, and his head pressed against her belly, listening for tiny cries, as if he could hear them. Pregnancy was supposed to bring them closer, but the claim he and the baby staked on her body drove her to mutiny, and her inexplicable moods drove him crazy.

The cliffs of La Jolla were deserted except for a few groups of pelicans moving about the edge. They studied the ocean, dozed, or aired their great wings. She leaned on the rusted metal railing and looked out. The grayish haze of the sky blended with the darker depths of the water, and it was hard to delineate where one ended and the other began. Below the horizon waves rose and fell in rhythm with the sea. She breathed in the moist ocean air and thought that inside her belly, water rocked and smelled of salty fish and seamen.

Off to her right a lone surfer paddled his way out to a crest. She had never learned to surf. When they had moved to the coast she'd thought that she was too old. Now she resented the fact that she couldn't, probably never would. She had once overheard an old surfer describe riding the waves as a moment when he became nothing more than a moving curl of water.

Evie imagined herself out on a surfboard, light and free, soaked with the salty spray of the ocean, her wet blouse plastered against the balloon-like belly, toes hanging over the board. Sliding down the wave.

A scuffing of footsteps broke her daydream. She heard them stop a few feet from her. Another day Evie might have felt fear, the fog was tangible and the cliffs deserted; but this morning she felt her protruding belly in some way protected her, and only glanced at the man in the tan overcoat.

After a few minutes he spoke. "This is the best time of the year for the ocean." His dark hair was graying at the sides and his jaw beginning to jowl, but he had the dark liquid eyes of a seal pup.

"Yes, my favorite." She stared out at the surfer.

"When I was a boy we used to ride our bikes down here. We spent all day playing in that cave over there."

She looked into his wet brown eyes and then followed his pointed arm to the entrance of the hollowed rock where the water rushed in, foamed and swirled, then retreated. He told her the stories and fantasies of his boyhood: shipwrecks, pirates, sea monsters, and mermaids. She saw the boy he'd been, clothes hanging from his skinny limbs, waving his stick in swordlike motions over a paper pirate's hat . . . his dark eyes dreaming. Evie wanted to touch him, stroke the brow over his soft pensive eyes, and smooth the graying hair. She felt a breathing between her legs. Caught off guard, she wasn't sure what was happening to her. She had to get out of there. "Well," she shoved her hands in her jacket pockets, "I have to go."

He ran his hand along the wet rail, then dried it on his overcoat, and nodded. "Take care."

Evie headed up the path to her car, concentrating on moving her legs evenly, not too fast, not too slow. He was a stranger; she didn't know him, felt nothing for him.

A few blocks up she found a small coffee shop, warm and smelling of yeasty breads. The young boy behind the counter handed her a steaming mug. Her eyes grazed along the curve of his fingers and up the silky brown-haired forearms covered with a light flour dust. He grinned at her. She clutched her mug and retreated to a corner.

Evie sat and sipped, staring out the window into the street. An occasional clang came from the kitchen. She thought of John again. They'd been married five years, and for five years she'd been happy in their bedroom, or living room, wherever they'd made love. So why now did her belly get in the way? And why had she felt drawn to that strange man on the cliff?

The solitary scrape of a chair unnerved her as the only other customer got up and left. She decided to call Joan and see if she wanted to have lunch.

The pavement was crowded with noon pedestrians. Suits strode alongside T-shirts and tennis shoes. Evie waited at the light behind a man with sandy hair tapering down the thick of his neck. The light turned and she followed his beige chinos across the street. A pair of square shoulders in a yellow polo shirt crossed the street from the opposite direction. Behind him followed a white button-down shirt, the bottom button stretched by the stomach behind it. A pair of blue jeans approached in a straight-hipped walk. Again, the breathing between her legs.

Evie paused on the other side of the street, overcome by the maleness surrounding her. She knew they carried a flesh between their legs, held snug against their lower bellies by their shorts. Blood pulsing through thin silky skin. She felt an urge to take them home; cradle them in the warm darkness of her arms.

Evie took a long breath, and started down the street. They should all wear kilts that showed their bony knees, and let it dangle. But that image didn't help much either.

When Evie arrived, Joan was already in the restaurant, drinking coffee and smoking a cigarette.

"How long have you been here?"

"Not long, but hurry up and decide, I'm starving."

Evie sat down and skimmed the menu. "What I really want is a hot fudge sundae on top of chocolate cake."

"Feeling pregnant, huh?"

"All boobs and belly."

They waited for their food, and Joan told Evie horror stories of being pregnant in hot sticky Texas. At six weeks she had puked in the 7-Eleven parking lot because she had gotten up too early. Months later her weight had broken a swing at their friend's barbecue. Everyone had gathered around, serious and concerned, but Joan had laughed so hard with embarrassment that she had thought she might go into labor. Soon after on the long trip to California, she'd had to pee so bad, and they'd pulled over onto the side of the road. Bill had held her so she wouldn't tip over, because she had no balance, like one of those toy Weebles.

Evie laughed until her cheeks hurt.

"Joan . . ."

"Yeah?"

"Did you ever feel . . . like you wanted to, well . . . that you were attracted to other men . . ."

"Always," Joan laughed.

"I mean all of them, no matter what they look like, or their age, or anything. Because you know there's this passion in them to be loved . . . mothered . . . and . . ."

"You'd need a lot of tits for that, Evie. You'd look like one of those fucking fertility goddesses, a thousand tits hanging off you." She laughed again, and fiddled with her spoon.

"Yeah." Evie stared down at her chest.

"But I know what you mean." Joan drew on her cigarette. "It's the mother thing. You can't always turn it off." She crushed out her menthol cigarette. "Now I want dessert."

They finished lunch with talk of stretch marks, labor pains, and midnight feedings.

Evie felt better, and when she got in her car to head back home, the sky had brightened. The sun had burnt off most of the morning haze, and the air was beginning to dry. She stopped at a nursery and walked among the rows of potted plants, running her fingers along the lengths of leaves, examining the white plastic labels. Someone had once given her a poinsettia at Christmas, but all its leaves had dropped off one by one, and she had decided then that she had a brown thumb.

The smell of jasmine drifted on a current, mingling with the smell of green and massaging her senses. A skinny man with a long face came out of the building and asked her if she needed help. His build and kindly demeanor reminded her of Mr. Green Jeans. She followed him over to the jasmine, smiling at the baggy pants that barely hinted at the curve of his butt.

They walked in and out among the plants, stopping to look at whatever caught her eye, and he told her how to care for them, what they needed in the way of sun or shade, water and nutrients, when they bloomed or became dormant. He carefully removed any dead leaves he came across, crumbled them in his fingers, and dropped them into their pots. "Most people throw them away, but I figure it makes a kind of compost, so the leaves go back and feed the roots." His wrinkled bony hand drew a circle in the air from leaf to root and back up.

She picked out a night blooming jasmine that would unfold yellow flowers in the evenings. She chose a wild rose bush with red petals that bloomed sparser and more delicate than the cultivated variety, and then a large, deep-green lacy fern. He loaded them into the car, and she thanked him for his help.

When Evie got home, she unloaded the plants and took them into the bathroom. Her mind drifted back to her conversation with Joan. She closed her eyes and imagined herself back in an ancient time when they performed fertility rites in the spring, sacred sexual acts, and the mother with "a thousand tits" nurtured all.

Evie picked a few fern leaves and scattered them across the tile. Then she clipped off a few stems from the wild rose bush and draped them around the bathtub. She cut some long strands from the jasmine, let her clothes drop, and circled the strands around her waist, looping the ends so they hung down beside the curve of her belly, tickling and scratching her skin. She took another vine and broke it in half, circling the pieces around her arms. Goose bumps rose to the surface of her skin and she laughed.

She felt ridiculous.

And elated.

Evie heard John's car drive into the garage, the door open, and John call her name. She felt a breathing between her legs, and turned on the bath water, smiling. ❦

What feels sensual and/or sexual to you pregnant? What aspect of your relation-ship with men has changed? How is "mother-energy" manifesting in your life?

Date _____

Alchemy

Deborah Bogen

At Laguna, I see little girls in their one-piece swimsuits, bottoms hanging out, sandy cheeks, and that frightening sense of purpose as they dig holes to fill with water for the poor sand crabs they have elected to love. And rising from the nape of my neck, from the very back of my brain, a picture interrupts this late afternoon, a slide out of order on the carousel. Suddenly you're here, six-years old, down at the water's edge in a blue spandex swimsuit, your red hair braided, your body lifting, on your toes to catch a seagull.

Which cell did what first, when I invited alchemy into my darkest room? Better to be the wafer than the priest if you want to study transubstantiation. Better to house knotted desires and think of how children build toy houses, one plastic brick at a time. Or is it like Mr. Potato Head—these eyes, this nose—till there's more than a marble bag of cells. I take long baths, read Dr. Spock, busy growing miles of new veins as the pear becomes the watermelon, as the fishy little gilled thing whispers, "Eat salt."

In the hotel dining room, I see a girl, eleven or twelve, her long hair capped by a French beret, at breakfast. She's elegant and gangly, Audrey Hepburn in the making, and begging her mother to let her have coffee—just this once.

Later I nap in the sun, dream that we drive you up to Santa Cruz, barely eighteen, all your worldly goods stuffed into a duffle bag, a flawless flashback to 1969 when I smoked dope and frequented hippie houses, playing hearts under the tutelage of LSD. How could I leave you with strangers in a house with bad plumbing, vegetarians, a whole tank of laughing gas in the living room? In the dream you laugh and say, "I'm fine, I'm fine," and remind me that you always knew you were meant to live by the ocean.

And today we're here in Laguna where I close my eyes against the glare and confuse the cries of seagulls and children as you reshape this big brown belly. Today I sense another pregnancy going on a long time. I see myself in someone else, a young girl moving constantly into the distance, becoming foreign, exotic, plane tickets stuffed into traveling bags, invitations to do soil work in Costa Rica or race 10Ks in Germany. The place you own in my body will migrate north until our linked hearts begin to alternate: "I'm here, I'm gone. I'm here. I'm gone."

In what ways has your relationship to children and babies changed? What places or landscapes are you consciously and unconsciously taking your baby in utero? *Why?*

Date _____

Quickening

Joanna C. Scott

*B*efore now, nothing. Just my face, dreaming,
Lily-pale, gazing back from those dark pools
Revealing not his soul but mine. Longings.
Urgings from a source beyond. Callings
From deep water. That no-sound sound
Above a lake in the split infinite minute
Between night and day. The white moon's
Face looks up. Sheer surface quicksilvers,

And almost close enough to touch, a ripple
Rises like a kiss from underneath. Love spreads
Silently, coming toward and going,
Edge-water yearning outward into reeds.
Around, a mirrored pulsing on the air
Like sobbing, like the beating of a heart. ✤

Describe what it's like to feel your baby moving inside you. What's the most surprising aspect? Reflect on any ways this inner motion has shifted your relationship to the baby, the outer world, or yourself.

Date _____

Little Miracle at the St. Anthony

Madeleine Mysko

At the door to the hotel room, Jenny searched through three compartments of her bag—both zipper pockets and the open pocket under the flap—before she remembered she had put the key in her wallet. The wallet, thank God, was where it was supposed to be, in the inside pocket. And yet her heart was pounding. Pure craziness—because so what if she had lost the key? They would give her another at the front desk, no questions asked.

The minute she stepped into the room, she kicked off her shoes, pulled back the covers, and lay facedown across the bed. She could feel her pelvis enfolding that hard roundness. She was well into her fourth month, but still that roundness came as a surprise—not so much that it was there, but more that it was a lot firmer than she'd imagined it would be.

"The uterus is a powerful muscle," Carrie, the midwife, had said. "The uterus has hard work to do." There was a poster in Carrie's office to illustrate—a uterus like a red fist, glistening muscles roped around every which way.

Jenny had gazed up at that poster and wondered how any child might be lost from such a powerful grip. And yet it happened all the time. As a matter of fact, it had happened to Jenny's sister three times. *Miscarriage.* A strange word—it seemed to lay the blame in the wrong place.

As for Jenny, there had been no such problem. As a matter of fact, with the exception of a little morning sickness, pregnancy had so far been as easy as one-two-three. She and Mark had conceived on the first try—a blessing which made Jenny uncomfortable around women like her friend Melissa in the office, childless women who had been trying so hard for years. One try, and lucky Jenny was cantering happily through the months, "healthy as a little horse," as her husband Mark liked to say.

Which was why they had decided that she ought to go ahead and attend the three-day conference—all expenses paid, at a fine old hotel in downtown San Antonio. Once the baby was born, Jenny wouldn't be so free. In fact, they had decided that once the baby was born, she would cut back to part-time and refuse to travel altogether, even if it meant changing jobs. So it would be good for her to enjoy this last trip. She had looked forward to it for weeks, and planned carefully—as she always did.

And yet, from the moment she arrived in San Antonio, she hadn't really been enjoying herself. The night before, she had lost her credit card—or, more precisely, had left it on the table in a restaurant, where fortunately the waitress remembered her mentioning the St. Anthony and called the desk immediately. In the morning she couldn't find her fountain pen, the really good one her mother had given her for her birthday. In the afternoon, while touring the city, she had gotten lost on the loop, the confusing access roads shunting her car from one interstate to another. She'd had to call the hotel for directions, her hands shaking, her voice stricken with that very hysteria she despised in other women.

St. Anthony, thought Jenny. *Patron saint of lost things*. It seemed she needed his intercession, a little miracle. For she had apparently lost her nerve.

She sat up and looked at herself in the mirror—the disheveled version of herself, the one with the chewed-off lipstick and the wilted bangs. It occurred to her that she might call Carrie. But what would she report? That she had a bad case of anxiousness? She already knew what Carrie would advise: get the feet up. Take a nap. Carrie hadn't been entirely in favor of the trip in the first place. "You don't want to tire yourself," Carrie had said. "You're carrying a child, you know, not just a couple extra pounds."

A child. She had lost the credit card and the pen—but she still had the child.

She called home.

"Having a good time?" Mark asked.

"Yes. Wonderful." She described the hotel. She told him about losing her way on the loop.

"I remember that," Mark said. He had once lived in San Antonio. "I can see how you'd get mixed up."

But she didn't tell him about the credit card, or the heart-pounding panic. She didn't want to worry him.

There was a dinner scheduled in the hotel dining room, an affair requiring something a little dressy. Jenny hadn't decided yet if she would wear the new dress she had packed—a tailored navy linen, her first real maternity dress. She wasn't really showing that much, and the extra drape might look frumpy. But she got up, slipped the dress from the hanger, and tried it on anyway. She was studying her profile in the mirror, rotating her hips to get the right effect, when there was a knock at the door. It was Mary Ann, a woman she had befriended at the conference the year before.

"Wow," Mary Ann said, stepping into the room. "I love the dress."

"But do you think it's too soon to wear it?" Jenny said, smoothing the pleats against her abdomen. "I mean I'm hardly showing."

Mary Ann settled her purse on the bed and sat down beside it. "Let me see," she said. "Walk over there to the window and back."

Jenny slipped on her shoes and walked to the window and back.

"Well, let's put it this way," Mary Ann said. "The women will definitely know you're pregnant. Especially from behind."

"Gee thanks," Jenny said. "I wasn't exactly thinking about the view from behind."

"Take it from me, sweetie. That view's going to be crucial for the rest of your life. But really—I'd wear it. People will make a fuss, and you might as well enjoy it. Unfortunately, it ends the day you get home from the hospital." She stood up and patted Jenny's shoulder. "You want to meet us downstairs? I'll save you a place at our table."

"Thanks," Jenny said. "I'll be down in a while."

"Take your time. They have cocktails first. You ought to get your feet up for a while."

After Mary Ann left, Jenny opened her bag to look for her lipstick. And there was the fountain pen, right in the bottom of the bag. If it had been a snake, it certainly would have bitten her.

The next day, when the afternoon session was over, Mary Ann and another woman, Toni from Pittsburgh, announced that they were going to take a stroll along the Riverwalk. Jenny said she'd go along.

"Are you sure you're up for that, little Mommy?" Toni said.

"I'll be fine." She was tired, but she didn't want to miss anything. She was thinking she could pick up some little souvenir. Perhaps a little something with St. Anthony on it, something to ward off the panic.

They walked three abreast the few blocks to the river, then descended single file into the crowds moving heavily along the narrow turns. The river was laden with tourist boats. A mariachi band serenaded them from the bridge. There were families everywhere—a father holding an infant to his chest with one broad hand and maneuvering the empty stroller with the other, a mother yanking a little boy back from the water's edge, children dashing ahead, ignoring their parents' calls. It seemed to Jenny that at any moment one of those children might slip from the pavement right to the bottom of that murky river, along which it seemed the entire population of the city was pushing its way.

"So many kids," Toni said. "Shouldn't they be in school?"

"Spring break," Mary Ann said. "This conference always coincides with spring break."

They passed an ice cream parlor. Outside, a frazzled-looking woman was doling out cones and paper napkins to three little girls. The youngest one was crying and stamping her feet.

"I'm sorry," the mother said. "But you know the rule." She didn't even look at the child, but settled herself wearily onto the bench.

The child kept wailing, butting her whole body against her mother's knees. Jenny wondered if she had been punished, refused an ice-cream cone—but no, there were three cones in all, one of which the mother was holding at arm's length and calmly allowing to drip onto the sidewalk.

Such scenes disturbed Jenny. She knew that if she were the mother she would have thrown that rule—whatever it was—to the wind, not only because she would hate the ruckus, but also because her heart would go to the child, who was obviously overtired. What did she want, this beautiful little girl with the damp curls and the fat tear-streaked cheeks? Perhaps a cone of a different color. Jenny was sure that if that were her child she would have gone back into the store for a cone of any color. But perhaps all the child really wanted was a nap.

It overwhelmed her all of a sudden, to think of the disciplining she would probably fail to do. She had felt the same way the first time she paged through a parents' magazine in the doctor's office. Though the photographs of the babies filled her with longing, she had a real aversion for the actual articles—food allergies, diaper rash, separation anxiety in nursery school—all that advice coming at her, demanding to be received.

They came to a little restaurant with tables on a terrace. A young man stepped forward from the shade and asked if the ladies would like a table.

"I could use a beer," Toni said.

"Me too," Mary Ann said.

But Jenny was tired. She urged them to go ahead without her. She reassured them she'd be all right. Then she headed for the hotel, pushing her hands into her pockets, touching the room key on the one side, and the wallet on the other.

Two blocks from the hotel she passed an antique store she hadn't noticed before. It was the woman in the display window that caught her eye—an older woman squatting down to wreath paper flowers around a badly chipped statue of the Virgin Mary. When Jenny went past, the woman stood up and smiled at her, and on impulse Jenny turned into the store. The woman stepped down from the window and took a seat behind the counter. She seemed disinclined to sell Jenny anything. There were no other customers, at least none whom Jenny could see.

It was a bigger store than one would have thought—deep rather than wide, and crammed with things not so much antique as old and quirky. Jenny lingered among the lawn ornaments—angels and Virgins, St. Francis in a full range of sizes—then wandered to the back, where the furniture was arranged into rooms, each one dimmer and mustier than the one before.

In the last room she discovered a peculiar collection of crosses fashioned from found items—weathered wood, rusted hardware, bent spoons and forks, scraps of tin. And at the foot of one of the crosses she spied a clay infant—probably a Nativity piece, although there was no halo, and the arms were not outstretched in the usual Baby Jesus fashion. He—or was it a she?—had been fashioned by someone who knew just how they wrapped a newborn in a receiving blanket in the hospital nursery. The clay infant was nearly a perfect replica of the newborns Jenny had seen through the nursery window, after the first prenatal class. All that was lacking was the clear plastic box with the identification in the slot.

She picked up the infant and closed her fingers over it. It fit perfectly into the palm of the hand, the little round head nestled just above the thumb. She remembered exactly how she had felt, standing there next to Mark, looking in at those babies in the nursery. She should have been delighted, but instead it had struck her that pregnancy had come to them too easily, much too quickly—before she'd really had a chance to be sure. And it was too late to go back. The feeling had taken her by surprise, and she had pushed it away, afraid that it might get through to their unborn child and work some harm. The same feeling had threatened to come over her more than once since then, and each time she had pushed against it in shame, for she and Mark had been blessed.

Suddenly the woman was there, smiling at her over the collection of crosses. "Isn't that just the cutest thing?" she said. "I sell those little babies as fast as they come in."

"Someone makes these for you?" Jenny looked down at the infant in her hand. She ran a finger along the sculpted folds of the blanket.

"Oh yes. A woman in Laredo. I think she ought to ask more for them myself."

"How much are they?"

"Ten dollars, I believe," the woman said. "Look on the bottom. Isn't that right?"

Ten dollars. The price was scrawled on the tiniest piece of masking tape on the infant's rounded bottom.

"I'll take it," Jenny said, handing the clay infant to the woman. "I love it."

The woman put her glasses on and looked hard at the baby. Then she peered over her glasses at Jenny. "You know we have a whole room of cribs and high chairs and such—upstairs, if you're interested."

"Thank you," Jenny said. "But I'm from out of town." She was taken aback. Was she really showing that much? Or had the woman seen something in her face?

The clay infant was more than a souvenir. It was a charm of some sort. The rest of the day Jenny carried it in her pocket, wrapped carefully in a wad of tissue paper.

At dinner she showed it to the others at the table.

"Adorable," Toni said.

"Precious," Mary Ann said, turning the infant over in her hand. "You'd better put it in a safe place—in your briefcase. You wouldn't want to lose it."

That night, Jenny set the clay infant next to her on the bedside table. She had trouble falling asleep. For hours she lay awake, every now and then turning over to gaze at that little round head glowing from the light in the bathroom—much like a nightlight she'd had as a child. Once she almost dozed off, thinking about the wallpaper in the room she had shared with her sister, and the sounds of her parents walking across the floor downstairs. But then suddenly, she was more awake than ever, and lonely.

It was too late to call Mark. Besides, she didn't want to worry him, didn't want him to know that she was afraid. So she took the clay infant into her hand then, and held it to her cheek. It was cold, of course—nothing but a figure, and no comfort to her in the dark. She put it back on the table and turned away. And that was when she first felt it, light and quick against that fist in her pelvis: the touch of the child—so delightful—the one who'd been with her all along.

As you become more obviously pregnant, how are people, especially at work, treating you differently? How is your own relationship to your work changing?

Date ____________

Magnificat

Chana Bloch

1
Now the fingers and toes are formed,
the doctor says.
Nothing to worry about. Nothing
to worry about

2
I will carry my belly to the mountain!
I will bare it to the moon, let the wolves howl,
I will wear it forever.
I will hold it up every morning in my ten fingers,
crowing
to wake the world.

3
This flutter that comes with me everywhere
is it my fear

or is it your jointed fingers
is it your feet

4

You are growing yourself.
out   of   nothing:
there's   nothing
at   last   I   can
do: I   stop
doing: you
are

5

Miles off in the dark,
my dark,
you head for dry land,

naked, safe
in salt waters.

Tides lap you.

Your breathing
makes me an ark. ❦

How do you experience the duality of all that you do (take prenatal vitamins, exercise, etc.) and don't have to do in order to grow this being? What has been your previous relationship to doing versus to being?

Date _____

Birth of a Woman

Ellen R. Klein

*I*t is this giving up of the self for the miracle of creating a child that I find so disconcerting. I am unsettled in my new role; no longer just a thirty-something career woman, now I will become someone's "Mommy." Make no mistake—I am loving my long-awaited, two-years-in-fertility-treatment pregnancy. I am in awe of the fact that within me lives a person who is the collective sum of all our ancestors. I am excited, elated, and euphoric.

And unsettled.

The physicality of this state is a no-brainer. Morning sickness, fatigue, weird food desires or aversions, not to mention the bulging breasts and stomach . . . all normal. Even, dare I say it, lovable. I love smoothing lotions across my belly, tenderly stroking that roundness and imagining a child beneath my hands delighting in the vibrations emanating from my hand. All of that is easy, happy, beautiful.

I hope I can pull it off.

I've lived a reasonably self-loving thirty-eight years without a child, and now that self-fullness will need to be shelved. Or will it?

What kind of mother can I aspire to be? Will I become so obsessed with diaper genies and Barney that I will have no mental reserves left over to spiritually feed my child? I can see the progression already; endless reading of *Your Week by Week Pregnancy* has taken over the morning time I previously spent devouring positive-thinking literature and books devoted to self-improvement. I'm so emotionally embroiled in our visits to the clinic and making sure that I'm doing absolutely everything to perfection, that I no longer give attention to my daily walks, writing time, and meditations.

I've cut off one life for another.

It has been my doing, not the embryo within.

Will I blame the child for other manifestations of this as the years parade past my window? Perhaps I will see what I am doing, right here and now, and affirm to be the sort of Mommy who:

1. loves herself as much as she does her child

2. is devoted to her child, of course, but remembers that the woman came first and that the woman has attendant needs

3. carves out personal time for herself and mate as well

4. remembers that there is plenty of love and nourishment to go around, and that resentment will only extinguish that love over time

This is very important.

I do not want to throw away thirty-eight years of my experience and personality. Rather, I want to share it happily and broaden it as well. This is a Herculean task, I know. Especially in the first few months of my child's life, I expect many tears, much sadness and difficult times.

But I have tremendous internal ammunition. If I can remember who I am, essentially, my infant will never be starved for a mother who can teach him the power of life, of eternity, of soul. My baby will know a mother figure who sings out loud, takes long beach walks with him at daybreak, and lies down with him on the floor surrounded by our animals, plants, and the love of a man as interested in spirit as I am.

My life is beautiful. It must continue to be.

These are my greatest gifts, the only possessions worth having in a world of shifting values and beliefs.

I know I can pull it off. ❧

What kind of mother do you aspire to be? Consider beginning with a list of aspects of your stereotypical image of a mother. Next, make a list of all that you will do for and not do to your future child. Finally, make a list of all you will do for yourself and not do to yourself as you integrate mothering (or mothering another one) into your former identity.

Date _____

The Age of Discovery

Joan Connor

*M*y hair wafts like kelp in water, a tangle of seaweed, a golden seine of pearls. Periwinkles cling to the strands. Water runs smooth over my stomach, a lover's cold hands. Above me waves crest, restless beneath the endless indifference of sky. I flash. A rush of bubbles beat like wings around my ears, and I break water and sing to you. Above the percussive boom of water against shore, the hush of drawing back, I sing to you. My hair slicks along my cheeks, my neck, my back like rockweed. My breasts crest the water, nipples taut with salt. The tide pushes my song to you, my song circling like seagulls, song soft as wind. You could swim into my song—or I could drop my song around you like a net and haul you in. I could wear your arms around my waist, an unending sash of love. You could swim into this song, these eyes, my eyes as green as dragon scales, as slippery as sin, that sheathe this fish tail hanging from my waist. Beneath the water line, my caudal fin, cold-blooded impossibility of love. But you could still risk loving me, could sing with me. My tail splashes sunlight. Follow me. Find my song growing from its roots, wedged like eelgrass in those rocks. You could risk loving me. I could show you Spanish gold, coral growing in orchards, pearls larger than your dreams, splitting the seams of rotted hulls. Hermit crabs will burrow in your sockets, snails make your bones their home. You could risk loving me. You would not be the first.

"Mary, Mary, are you still among the living?"

She blinked her eyes open. She was lying on her back. The fog, pressing so close against her, felt as if it were condensing on her skin from within. She sat up and smiled at Keith, smiled at his confounded eyes. He was worried, she knew. He'd been worried for months now, but there really was nothing she could do. Nothing.

"Would you like a hard-boiled egg?" she asked.

She watched Keith smack the egg against the rock. The shell crinkled as he rolled it beneath his palm. He peeled the shell off in bits, let them drop among the splinters of mussels, clamshells, the papery shells of tiny crabs, spineless sea urchins, beautiful as ring boxes, but broken, unhinged, smashed open on the rocks. Mary liked to see Keith's eggshells in the debris. The seagulls' picnic, she thought. She had seen the gulls tirelessly swoop down and soar again, almost in one single motion, fluid, with mussels or clams clamped in their beaks, rise high, higher, wings whipping the air into a froth, then drop the shells, smashing them, spilling their meat, and swoop again, swoop down— just a continuum of motion—to eat. She liked to picnic here. It was so natural.

"Are you warm enough, Mary?" Keith asked.

She nodded. He used her name frequently now. Reality therapy. Today is Wednesday, August eighth. Your name is Mary . . . or perhaps he used her name to stake his claim, to reclaim her, call her back to him as if one could own something by naming it. She laughed aloud, startling herself, startling Keith.

"Are you OK, Mary?" he asked, his brown eyes squinting with concern. "Are you OK?"

"I'm OK," she said. But she was drifting away again. She knew it. The long, ineluctable drawing back as natural as a tide responding to the tug of the moon, the wiles of wind. She watched Keith vanish, diminished by growing distance. Those sad eyes—points in space, empty space, mere holes. She couldn't do a thing about it. It was only natural.

Keith wasn't comfortable with nature. He never had been. Some years ago they'd had a dog. Fuzzy. A happy little mutt, docile, dozy . . . rather stupid, really.

✿

The year of the big snowstorm. Living in western New York then, very flat country, you could look forever ahead and behind you as if you could see through time in this landscape where space was time, where both were just the distance between two points. Snow filling space, filling time. The plows pack the snow into walls of ice, miniature mountains. On into dusk the rurr of the plows muffled by snow. Silence falls with night. Sudden. And as suddenly, as if a hand had drawn back a curtain, brilliant light. One moon, full moon, becomes a million moons reflecting off the icy crust, shattering darkness with the hard, adamantine edges of frozen light. I let Fuzzy out the kitchen door—he's been inside for days—and watch him skate over the crust of snow. I shut the door.

"What's that?" Keith asks. "What's that?"

A low growl at first, a yip, then a howl rising in perfect crescendo, ritual wailing, ululation. I draw back the curtain of the kitchen window. Fuzzy crouches atop a bank of snow, his head thrown back, his neck bared to the knife edge of moon. Ah-oo-oo. Some atavistic voice in his throat, his blood. I hear it with my spine.

"What does it mean?" Keith asks. "What's he doing?"

"Nothing," I say. But I think it is something like magic. I'm comfortable with magic. It's only natural.

✿

"Mary, are you OK? Are you in pain?" Keith fidgeted at her side. She felt the warmth of his hand around her wrist like a bracelet, loose, at first, a bangle, then tightening into a cuff. She must have howled out loud. She'd always had an energetic imagination, a whimsical memory. Scenes would come back to her, take substance from nothing, from air, and crowd out the present. But lately her body as well as her mind relived those memories, jerked through a reenactment: hands fluttering, words gurgling, tears—a reflex mechanism. But she wasn't really sad. She wasn't really anything at all. She felt Keith grip her wrist.

"Are you hungry?" he asked. "Would you like a sandwich?" She felt her head shaking. "Something to drink?" Her head shaking again, her hair whipped against her face.

"I'm just tired," she said, and she smiled. She could feel how thin the smile looked on her face, lips stretched tight as rubber bands. The snapping point.

"Of course you're tired," he said and smiled too near her face. She could feel his smile reflected in her eyes, two shallow bowls. She shut her eyes. "Maybe you should lie down," he said. But he did not release her wrist, as if he were insisting on his bond with her, this bond of flesh. She twisted her wrist and felt his fingers surrender her. She pressed her back against the sea grass, the rock.

It was remarkable, really, how little he had to do with her, with this, she thought, her palms cupping the firm swell of her belly. Even she'd been surprised. It had nothing to do with him, and sometimes, almost angrily, she'd felt how little it really had to do with her.

At first she'd felt she'd been invaded. The *Invasion of the Body Snatchers*. She'd eaten foods she'd never cared for. Clothes clung like a stranger's to her body. She'd kept odd hours, thought thoughts that weren't her own. She'd felt as if she were drowning, disappearing. This tiny life was swallowing her up. One night she'd started laughing; she was choking with laughter.

"What is it?" Keith had asked her, smiling, "What's so funny?" She couldn't breathe. She hugged her knees. "What's the matter?" he yelled, alarm cracking through his amusement.

"You're the pod," she'd panted. "Don't you see? You must be the pod"—tears ran down her face—"the pod I slept with." Water poured down her face. Saltwater. Keith didn't get the joke.

As she had crumbled saltines one morning into a bowl of milk, mashing them into mush, a cartoon image had impressed itself in dots, palpable as fingertips, against her eyelids. A pointillist fish being swallowed by a bigger fish being swallowed by a bigger fish being swallowed . . . the image lingered. And, after that, her alienation from it—she still thought of the baby as a thing, a presence not really human—hadn't mattered much any longer. Sometimes she wondered if she were carrying it at all. Perhaps it had floated away, dissolved. Only her nausea, the tight skin on her belly reminded her: I am here. I am here.

It was there. Always there. And she resented it, resented being a vessel, a container. She'd thought being a parent meant something active, muscular, sensible. Once, she'd almost pitied Keith, realizing how much more parenthood must be remote for him—an idea, but less than an idea—eclipsed, an idea cast in shadow. Umbra. She did not know exactly when she had become reconciled to, if not motherhood, the isolation of it. But she had begun to think of herself as a center of gravity, a swirl of gases, series of random chemical reactions defining a world that by chance rather than choice rocked a sea, an amniotic sea, breeding, generating a primitive evolution: amino acids, protozoa.

When she'd first learned of her pregnancy, she'd shown Keith a photograph, *The Stages of Development*, an embryo in utero. Curled and helpless, it resembled a human less than a seahorse. Seahorse, hippocampus. Keith had recoiled from the plate. He'd imagined the embryo as doll-like, a miniaturized adult, perhaps even fully clothed, ambulatory. She wasn't certain; she hadn't asked. They hadn't discussed the child much since their initial arguments over names.

Keith had favored Standish, but she'd preferred a name more remarkable for its ordinariness, like David or Michael. Keith's preference for polysyllabic feminine names discouraged her. So long a name for one so small: Henrietta, Victoria, Anastasia. But that was before he'd seen *The Stages of Development*. He hadn't mentioned names since. They never had agreed upon one. Mary no longer cared. She imagined that eventually the name, like the child, would spring forth as naturally as Aphrodite from the sea. Born from sea foam. The froth of words, of names. Mere evanescent air. She sank into a prelingual world of half-formed connections, as if she were forgetting the relationships between ideas and words, objects and names, an intricate circuitry fizzling away. But she felt no loss; it was only natural. Natural as air.

Keith pressed a paper cup into her hand. "To all the good men lost at sea," he toasted, arm upraised to the ocean rolling somewhere behind the drape of fog. Mary sat up.

"I think the fog's lifting," Keith said. "You can almost make out the bell buoy now." He shaded his eyes as if there were sun and squinted in the direction of the sound. The bell had a low, full tone. An old sound, salt-eaten, Mary thought, resonant with age, experience. I have always been here, it tolled, I will always be.

"Yup, it's fairin' up," he said dropping his *g*, a mannerism he'd developed his first summer on the island. Mary supposed he thought it sounded more like "Maine talk."

Keith grew up in the Midwest. His childhood, as he described it, always seemed beyond him, a brighter, better place he longed for, as he stared between the slats of a metaphoric picket fence, hoping for a peek. He still longed to push outward, forge ahead. Silicon Valley, the job market of the future, the lure of the Californian coast. But he had settled for her ocean, her summer island, suppressing his wanderlust for her. She did not want to move anywhere. She never had longed for a someplace else. She had been content with her memories, the ritual of opening and closing the cottage, family picnics, her bell: I have always been here; I will always be. So she tolerated Keith's affectations, his Maine talk. She rarely noticed it anymore. She sipped at her apple juice.

"Wouldn't you hate to be out in this?" Keith asked. She nodded. "It really makes you respect those guys who sailed over here from Europe, doesn't it? No radio, electronic devices. Just the stars. Amazing."

"Amazing," she echoed, but she was not thinking about exploration. She was not thinking at all.

"Do you think they'll ever find that poor guy?" Keith asked. "Mary?"

She shook her head. "I'm sorry, I wasn't listening." She smiled at him, set down her paper cup. "What did you say?"

"Do you think they'll find that guy, the one who set off from Portland to cross the ocean single-handed?"

Yes, she remembered. Lost at sea. Topical references were another of Keith's strategies to keep her oriented to the present, to events. Louis Clark set out on Wednesday, August first, from the Portland waterfront on a single-handed, trans-Atlantic sail. He never got past Portland Head Light. The Coast Guard found the empty sailboat, the fiberglass hull neatly halved, pounding against the ledges of Outer Green Island. A severe northeaster had blown in that afternoon and persisted into the night. They had not recovered the body. Facts. She did not think facts got you very far. And events had a habit of slipping away from you. Like her wedding with Keith—it had seemed so important at the time, but what had it really meant after all: a parade, some music, food and drink? And how did the facts explain why Louis Clark would attempt such a crossing in the first place? No, she had an instinctive distrust of facts and their coy ignorance of their own limitations. She wondered why men like Clark were always pushing outward in some dissatisfied quest for discovery, for something external, beyond their reach. Tantalus bending to drink the waters receding before him; but the thought dissolved as she pursued it. Keith's hand rested on her thigh.

"I hope they find his body for the family's sake," Keith said, patting her leg gently. "I guess Saint Nicholas wasn't watching out for Clark." He looked at her with a tenderness that surprised her, and, for a moment, she thought he was going to rest his head against her stomach. But he seemed to think better of it, or perhaps he was distracted by the gong of the buoy. Just a sound isolated in fog.

Keith's reference to Saint Nicholas struck her as odd; he was not a superstitious man. He had probably borrowed the allusion from Cappy, an island friend and a merchant marine. According to Cappy, Saint Nicholas was the patron saint of sailors and children. Both at sea from birth to death, he joked. But he took his superstitions seriously. Whenever he shipped out, a gold hoop glinted from his left ear, protection against drowning. She never doubted the power of that charmed circle of gold, but Keith scoffed at the notion—although never in Cappy's presence. He admired Cappy.

Keith was toying with the wedding band on her right hand. "We've come a long way, haven't we, Merry Mary?" He squeezed her hand.

She smiled. His question didn't expect an answer. Merry Mary, his pet name. She hated it, twisted it into Beriberi whenever he spoke it. But she kept her version of the nickname to herself perhaps out of a need for a secret, for some privacy, perhaps in respect for her mother's one bit of premarital advice. Keep some things to yourself, she had said, and for good reasons too. Leave a little mystery; don't chatter his awe away with his ear. What you withhold can make him need you. And try to keep your petty peeves to yourself. That way you'll never be a nag, and, when you do have a complaint, he'll listen. Wise advice, no doubt, but general advice of that sort always seemed to hover over specific situations, uncertain of its applicability. She wondered when and what to withhold. And her mother herself never acted on her own advice. She was a chatterer, a wonderful chatterer, overstuffed with words, as comfortable as an easy chair. Patent motives and expressed desires. And, no withholder, she gave and gave until you wondered why she didn't turn inside out with her own generosity. But perhaps she did reserve some of herself. The profundity of her charity only made her seem inexhaustible.

Mary's father struck her as more of a withholder. He blushed whenever he kissed his daughter. He liked the contact, she thought, but his emotions embarrassed him. Still, she knew he loved her; she had never doubted it. They'd evolved a symbolic language that both intuitively understood. They went on long, almost formal, walks together, and they were journeys into intimacy; their talk was a form of touching. Her father would speak of Tolstoy's special relationship with his daughter, and the story curled around her like an arm around a waist. Or he might talk about his own nearly mystical love of nature. Every leaf, he said, was the incontrovertible evidence of God's being. And she knew she was included in that love. Whereas the power of her mother's love derived from its chatty repetition, her father's derived from its very ineffability.

Sometime after she'd met Keith, she and her father had stopped going for walks. They had never discussed it—a complicity of silence. But she had missed, and perhaps she even still missed, those walks. The years they lived in western New York, she and her father would drive out to the lake, and follow, side by side, the path through the pines, so closely overgrown, it extended like an aisle to the shore. And then they would skirt the shore, the lake, so immense, it rested like a blue bar, like an altar on the horizon. But she could hear its restlessness, the lake's body surging with surf like the sea. As they walked, her father stooped occasionally to retrieve a shard of sea glass for his collection. He favored the cobalt blue, the rarest color. When his pockets bulged, he slipped the glass into her pocketbook, which was always gritty with sand. Her mother had snuck the bell jars of sea glass off to the dump years ago. Mary missed their kaleidoscopic patterns dancing in sunlight on the kitchen floor. Her father rarely went out walking now.

But both her parents were pleased about the baby. It would be their first grandchild. Her mother had oohed and aahed, bought teddy bears and bassinets and blankets dotted with baby ducks. Her father had spoken solemnly of blood, continuity, the hedge against death. And he had spoken of his father: "When my father first came to this country from Ireland, he was only a gardener, a dirt-poor potato farmer. . . ." He usually introduced his father in this way, but the stories that followed were always new, fresh.

She remembered when her grandfather had died. Good Friday. Her father wanted to get away from the wake, to breathe. They'd driven up to the lake. They walked so hushed, so stately through the pines to the water, that she ceremoniously took her father's arm. As they worked their way up the beach, she thought she saw her father crying. But it's only the air, she thought, still raw, still cruel with winter. But when her father bent over to pick up shards of glass, his movements were furtive, embarrassed. He was crying. "My father was a quiet man," he said. "He kept to himself. And I wish, I only wish . . ." he clenched his fistful of seaglass ". . . I had taken more time with him, more time to know him."

I had never heard Dad speak so directly from his pain. I do not know where to rest my eyes, so I look at his hand. And he looks at his hand. We cannot raise our eyes to each other. And slowly the hand relaxes, reveals this trash, broken bits of Coke bottles, Noxema jars ground against the sand until, polished by time, they glitter quietly, perfect gems. I touch the heel of my father's palm. "These are not ready yet," he says and sprinkles bits of the glass into the palm of my hand. Then he turns his back, and, throwing against the wind, tosses them into the lake. I'm crying, and I throw mine into the wind too, scattering them like so much ash . . .

"Mary," Keith yelled. His hands held her shoulders. His hair sparkled with flecks of eggshells and clamshells. "Stop it."

She stared at the grit of shells, sea urchins in her hands. He shook her violently, yelling, "You're behaving like a lunatic, a goddamned lunatic. What's the matter with you? Talk to me." His mouth was so close to her face, she felt the warm rush of air, his words, as if he were trying to breathe their meaning into her. Artificial respiration. "What is the matter with you?"

"I don't know," she nearly whispered. The bell buoy rolled with a wave, tolling. When they'd come down early last summer for a picnic, a baby seal, umbilical cord still attached, watched them from the base of the buoy. The mother seal circled, never far off, watching the seal watch them. Mary tried to wriggle out of Keith's grasp, out of his stare.

He let her go, but his words rushed at her, encircling her. "You're using the pregnancy to shut me out. I can't take this, this silence anymore. I've tried to understand, but I cannot understand this—Mary, Mary? What are you doing? Mary?"

She stood up, brushing shells and crumbs from her jeans. A boat passed near them in the fog, so near she could hear the crackle of its radio, the mumble of voices. Lobstermen hauling their traps most likely. Eerie having them so near and yet unseen. "I'm going for a walk," she said. "I need to be alone for a while."

"It's unfair. Unfair, Mary." Then, "Mary, come back here. Come back here now." But the words dropped behind her on the rocks. "You'll hurt yourself. You shouldn't be climbing in your condition. Mary . . ." Her name blended with the wind, the waves. Mar-eee, so natural.

As she picked her way carefully along the rocks, she thought of the walks with her father along the lake. They had never discussed it, but she suspected they both had felt the lake to be a pale, landlocked imitation of the ocean they walked along in the summer. On the island, it was almost as if the ocean walked around them. More powerful than the lake, more primitive in its power, the sea ate away at the island; salt pecked away at rusty car bodies, wore shingles down to gray; winds twisted the pines into hunchbacked gnomes; the bite of the water chomped on the pilings, rain peeled the paint off houses. You had to respect power like that. Her father did, and his mother had before him. She'd grown up in County Mayo on the ocean. Her eyes were blue, she said, dyed from watching the water day after day for her brother Martin's boat. He was a fisherman who dropped his net once too often. It tangled him up. He never came back. But, her grandmother said, the ocean could be beautiful as well as harsh. When she fell asleep at night, she could see from her bedroom window the boats moored off the point. The lights aboard ship twinkled on at dusk until the sea reflected an enchanted city, a fairy city lit with a million candles, bobbing on the water as brilliant as a netful of stars, the purity of wishes. Mary had not, perhaps, inherited her grandmother's poetry, her longing, but, like her father, she had inherited her grandmother's love of the ocean. She'd been rocked in it since her childhood, since her family first started coming up to the island in the summers. Over thirty years now. So much time.

A cormorant flew overhead, and she shuddered involuntarily. She'd always hated them, feared them even though she knew they were harmless. Their serpent necks, yellow reptilian eyes, black pterodactyl wings. Their eyes missed nothing. The fishermen called them garbage birds. They were skilled and greedy hunters. Cappy sometimes recited a saying about them, how they could drink the ocean for an aperitif, gnaw a continent to the bone, swallow the universe, and ask for an appetizer. The cormorant veered away, his wing a parenthesis erased by fog.

She looked around for a spot to sit down. She tired more quickly now with the added weight to carry. Her heaviness still surprised her—that a thing so small could make her feel so earthbound. Even her ankles had swollen as if to anchor her to the ground. She'd felt it, the baby, move once, or she thought she had. A fluttery sensation like a butterfly brushing against her from within—light as the opal dust on its wings, substanceless as a kiss. The moment had snuck up on her, surprised her, launched her into the air, skywriting her elation. And then nothing. It hadn't stirred since.

Mary picked up a piece of driftwood and poked at the seaweed in a tidal pool near her feet, startling a hermit crab who burrowed back into its borrowed shell. Poking through the pools fascinated her—a tiny world thriving in spite of its abandonment by the larger world. Sea urchins, snails, barnacles—it bored Keith silly. Most of the things she enjoyed bored Keith silly, but he was a good sport about it.

The summer before she and Keith had been married, she'd begged him to take her to the Holley Fair. He had. He even accompanied her to the palm reader's trailer among the porta-toilets on the outskirts of the fairgrounds. She'd appreciated it, because she knew he'd rather be at the Test Your Strength booth, readying the muscles in his back for the heft of the mallet.

They'd found the trailer crouching beneath a huge wooden sign of an unblinking eye, "Madame Hier. Palm reading. Astral Projection. Destiny Consultant." They'd knocked on the screen door and stepped into the hot, close darkness, the air, heavy with cats who perched everywhere—on the Coleman stove, on the toppling piles of cartons, the furniture crowding the narrow room. Litter boxes overflowed onto the floor.

"What smell?" a voice asks itself and laughs. A lump of a woman, knobby and hunched, appears above a tower of cardboard boxes. Her duster is so stained and spotted that the print is no longer discernible. "Company, kitties," she says and shuffles toward the cats as if walking were painful. Her fuzzy, pink slippers flop softly against the floor as she scuffs nearer. Shup, shup. Her stockings, rolled down to her calves, look like doughnuts on her legs. She wheezes, and mutters, and gasps, stumps of teeth in her gums. And her eyes peer ahead as if trying to see through the milkiness of her cataracts. She brushes at cat hair flying around her nose and sneezes.

"What do you want?" she asks leaning forward. "Huh? Cat got your tongue?" Her laughter sounds like choking. She tilts nearer. Her hair tufts like a cat's fur after a fight. The crown is bald. "What do you want?" she asks again.

Keith grins. "You're the fortune teller. You tell us."

She snatches at my hand and reels me in closer to her. I can smell the decay: the sweet rot of teeth; skin drying out, curling like paper. "I can help you, Mary," she hisses. My tongue falls numb in my mouth. Her hand strokes mine. A picture taped to her forehead—a man, a man in a cap, no, Christ crowned with thorns—looms forward. "Oh, you're pretty all right," she purrs and rubs her cheek against the back of my hand. "But don't you work the devil with it, you deceiver, harlot. Delilah!" she shouts in my face. I jump. My back runs with water.

And Keith is laughing. He doesn't understand magic. He has no fear. I want his heart to pump ice water like my own. But he is mocking, laughing. "You tell her, Grandma," he says. And she smiles sightless in his direction. His face glows red and healthy in the heat. His hair curls in black coils. I can feel the strength of the cords in his neck. They tie me up, bind me so helpless before his beauty.

"You will marry and have many children, but beware of water . . ."

"Mary's a common name," Keith said later, "and everything else the old lady said was so general it could have applied to anybody." Lucky guesses and formula fortunes. But she hadn't been convinced. Looking ahead like that made her dizzy. Keith loved to look ahead, took great anticipatory leaps: technology will answer the problems of technology; the ocean is the lower forty of the future. He liked to read sci-fi. Dizzying. She felt a little faint.

A starfish unfurled its legs in the tidal pool. One, two, three, four. The fifth was missing, but she thought she remembered hearing somewhere that they could regenerate their limbs. Five legs like five fingers. She looked at her hand. Stars in the ocean, stars in the sky. She trembled. Something, a seed of an idea, germinated, took hold. So much pattern. Connections. Phosphorescent water, a comet in the sky, pelagic glimmer. She suddenly felt the vast connectedness of sea and soil and sky, of rock and bone, and her place in an immense design. Looking down into the tidal pool, at its barnacled rock basin, all evolution struck her as no more than layer after layer of sediment, metaphoric accretions, each stratum a history. She knew, she had always known, that the explanation for the present could be exhumed from the past. But history, she realized, the past, was not static. The idea leaped at her: history was an impulse toward completion, a pressing forward to a destiny that might have no witnesses, but that, once begun, surged forward on its own momentum. She was panting, borne forward by the thought, buoyed up. Ideas crowded into her mind—an unruly crowd gawking at a carnival of lights.

And she remembered lining up, veiled in white before the Mother Superior, catechized for the last time before her First Communion. Who made you? God made me. The Mother Superior, a black tower, peering down at them, the children, as she explained that childbirth was God's punishment for original sin. Adam and Eve. And perhaps the centuries and all of their events from the smallest sigh to the largest war could be explained by just one woman and one man. Myth, religion, science dropped like nets over a simple biological design and knotted from the same fibers—the blood fear, birth pain, lust, bone weariness—they strained to restrain. All civilization, one vast metaphor which struggled to deny its analogous origin, its physiological conception, even while it offers its deepest expression. A literary disguise for this bone, this drop of blood. This heartbeat and that heartbeat, the plangent slap of water against shore. This breath, that rush of wind, in and out, an endless, all-inclusive circling. But, as she strove for the similarities, they turned against her, taunting. All the same. All the difference. All the same. She wrestled with the words, tried to prod them into an orderly line of thought, but she felt the lucidity fading, pulling back, casting her in uncharted waters, the familiar solitude of futile thought. Just the boom and boom and booming of the waves. A rhythm meaning nothing, leaving her beached.

When she at last lifted her eyes from the tidal pool, she thought the fog appeared to be dispersing. Like a bride lifting her veil, she thought. But the simile promised too much, more like a ghost shredding its own shroud—nothing tearing nothing to tatters. Boom, boom, boom. Swash, swash, swash. The tattoo of the surf tapped out triplets, singsong, the rhythms of doggerel verse or child rhymes.

Down by the seashore, down by the sea,
Johnny broke a teapot and blamed it on me.

Or the tag ditty the island children sang:

Chop, chop, chop with a butcher's knife,
Stuffed in a barrel of salt.
Who would have thought Saint Nicholas
Could bring three boys back to life.
Pickled in the brine.
Pickled in the brine.
Circle round three times three for nine.
Break in ahead of the butcher man.
Circle round once, and you're whole again.
Boom, boom, boom.

She wondered if Keith was still waiting for her at the picnic spot. Perhaps he'd hiked back to the cottage, discouraged beyond patience, or he might be skipping stones, competing with himself for one more step skimming out over the water. Why hadn't he come after her? This time had she gone too far—walking away from him in the fog? But the fog was lifting. She was certain of it now. She could see the point of the cove and the rocks along the breakwater. A shape huddled on the rocks in the spray of waves along the shore. A seal perhaps or a mermaid. Amphitrite. Boom, boom, boom . . .

You might have asked me. You could at least have asked before you stole me away from my ring of Nereids, my island of Naxos. I was young there and happy. But I would still have come, Poseidon, my hair coiled in a net to wear your crown, my diadem of crab claws. I would still have come riding dolphins bareback through the waves. You might have asked. Were you afraid that like Proteus I'd twist myself into a wave, dive into it, a slippery seal, surface for a breath of air, and breathing it, become it, and sough away, away from you? No, I would still have come to you, the Nereids' perfect music in my ears, and not turned back. I only wish you'd asked, just asked, asked once.

The bell buoy gonged. Her back hurt. She wanted to go home now. But would Keith be ready to forgive her, to welcome her back? He might need more time to soothe his anger, or his hurt. She would walk down the bank first to the water's edge, dawdle a bit before heading back, let him miss her.

As she neared the shore, the fog seemed to crawl away before her. It moved but imperceptibly, unobtrusively, like some hunted thing not wishing to call attention to itself. "Fairin' up," Keith would say. The shape on the rocks shifted as she approached. A seal, she thought again. She wondered how close she could get, how long she could take advantage of its curiosity.

As she tacked toward the shore rocks, she watched her feet choose their way carefully over the loose rock and debris wedged in the crevices of the ledges. Battered slats of lobster traps, a chunk of a cork float, the cracked scoop of a child's plastic shovel. She homed in on the seal almost instinctively, scanning the rocks for it only occasionally. Yes, it was still there. She picked her way gingerly, carrying herself like a china cup brimful of precious liquid, aqua vitae. She couldn't bear to trip now, to startle it back into the too ready water. Move like fog, she thought. She wanted to see its eyes, those dark, wet eyes. A rubber glove missing a finger, a Budweiser can, its letters nearly bleached out, almost illegible. Still there. Still there. She wanted to see its eyes, and the want throbbed through her like blood. Although she knew it was crazy, she could not squelch the feeling that the seal had become the fulcrum on which everything balanced. Everything depended on seeing the seal; she had to see the seal. Its skin felt as natural to her as her own. She could feel water play along her sides, her brow wrinkling as she plunged down, down, colder and darker. To see the seal. Just a few more yards . . .

But it wasn't a seal after all, she thought, close enough now to detect a patch of orange. It wasn't a seal but still something alive, a . . . it raised its head.

A bloated, half-eaten, pickled, blubbery thing blew at her the smell of death. I'm going to blow you a kiss, it said, wordless, eyeless, gaping at her—a lipless mouth. My rotted lips puff between yours, in and out; the life goes in or out. Just a dark grinning hole. A kiss. Her eyes snapped shut, opened again scrambling for understanding, for something else to see. Stuffing spilled from a gash in the life jacket. Still there. At her feet a hermit crab burrowed backward into a rubber doll's arm. I'm going to blow you a kiss, it said again. The life jacket bobbed in the tide washing up onto the rocks, lifting the head, that endless tunnel of mouth promising, I'll suck you in. Suck. You. In.

She felt the scream before she heard it, felt it for years. And, until she heard it, she wondered whether she'd been struck deaf or mute. The word she finally heard surprised her. "Keith!" she yelled, "Keith!" finding a name where only fear had been. And in that instant the baby kicked, not fluttered, but kicked, kicked hard. "I'm getting out of here one day," the feet pounded.

And Keith called back to her. "Mary!" he yelled. Her name grabbed her like a fish hook. Mary. Almost visceral, the name digging into her flesh.

His fingers clamped around her wrist hauling her in. She knew then he'd followed her. He's been nearby all along, she thought. Keith tugged her arm, turning her away from it, the body. Louis Clark, she suddenly knew its name, and for a minute she struggled to slip away, wriggle like a fish, eel from Keith's hands, snake into the water—I leave you with only the iridescence of fish scales on your hands, the memory of the smell of salt . . .

But he was gathering her to him, his left hand tightening around her wrist. "Hush. Don't think about it, Mary. It'll be all right." Keith gripped her. The baby kicked. She gasped for air. The pressure of changing elements. And she realized the swell in her stomach meant more than having a baby. It meant having a mother, having a father. Yes, she said to the pressure on her wrist, fingers tight on her pulse, having a husband. The whole charmed family circle like a clearing in the woods where witches bond in blood at night. The whole fam-damily, as her mother said. And when her eyes met Keith's, the familiar brown, the tender look that pulled her in, the look she knew she would remember from that moment on as the birth of their family, she wondered if she would ever forgive him.

Keith nudged her gently in the direction of the picnic spot. "We should get back and call someone," he said. "His people will want to know we've found his body."

At their feet, unnoticed, a hermit crab's claws poked cautiously from a doll's arm, testing the rocks as if they rested on the edge of world. Mary turned her back to the water. ❀

Reflect on your feelings of connection to and distance from your baby, nature, and/or other people. What is your relationship to the "facts" of your pregnancy? If you have one, how is your relationship with your partner unlike what you thought it would be during this period of gestation?

Date _____

The Mother Connection

Hope Edelman

*I*t rained the day of my grandmother's funeral, a fine drizzle that clung to our dark coats like a silver veil. She died this past December, a few weeks short of her ninetieth birthday. We buried her in the family plot just behind my mother, who died at forty-two. The official documents listed my grandmother's cause of death as acute respiratory and coronary failure, backed up by advanced breast cancer—an absolute calamity of the chest—but I believe otherwise: despite all her ailments, she died of loneliness and quite possibly a broken heart. She kept asking for my mother until the very end.

The bonds between mothers and daughters have always been tight in my family—too tight, most of us have complained. It's as if the women believe that the harder they cling, the more they can protect. If only that were true. Our stories are marked by departure and longings, by frustration and despair. My great-grandmother Ida, leaving Russia at 36 with three children, saying goodbye to the mother she would never see again. My grandmother Faye, a stubborn, willful woman with a love so enduring and irrational that it often drove my mother to slam down the telephone or retreat into her bedroom to scream at the walls. My own mother, whose early death from breast cancer left behind two angry teenage daughters and a mother who walked around for months refusing to accept—was never able to accept—the truth.

In the full Bonwit Teller shopping bags my grandmother used to carry wherever she went, she kept a framed photograph of her mother, a serious woman in a dark print dress, who died before I was born.

I used to laugh at her for this, teasing her for dragging around a picture of an old woman in the bottom of a tattered paper bag. My mother would hush me, telling me to leave Grandma alone. Only later did I realize the poignancy of this act, how important those bags were to my grandmother's feelings of safety and well-being, and how the image of her mother must have provided the same; how my mother understood this and how by gently quieting her daughter she showed loyalty to an aging mother who at other times nearly drove her mad.

I treasure these memories now, along with the stories these women told me about their lives. As we sat around the kitchen table or took long drives in the car, they handed down women's culture, replete with all its tales of hardship and triumph, loss and rebirth. My grandmother spoke of her mother's ability to stretch a piece of meat far enough to feed seven, and about how she herself studied to become a lawyer only to find she didn't have enough money for the exam fee. My mother told stories about maturing faster than her peers, about how her mother hadn't prepared her for menstruation and how she swore, at age nine, that she would tell her daughter in advance. (She did, when I was eight.)

But now there is no one left who can verify my memories of these women, who heard the exact stories they told me, or can add to them, or tell me which details I've got wrong. At thirty-two, I'm the only woman left in my maternal line, and few things I've encountered have made me feel quite so alone.

I was acutely aware of this as I stood at my grandmother's grave in the gentle rain. Damn it! I wanted to cry out. The last one gone! I understood that I represented a symbolic end point, but I did not yet realize I could represent a beginning, too. So it is perhaps not all that surprising that when I learned I was pregnant, less than two months after the funeral, I received the news with uncharacteristic calm. It was a statistical fluke, one of those birth-control failures that pull effective rates down into the ninety-odd percentiles, or so the gynecologist said. I didn't disagree. In the frenzy that followed—planning a wedding, buying a house, and all those doctor's visits—there wasn't much time to sit and reflect. Which is probably why I didn't notice for months that this year I'm bridging the gap between death and birth. I've lost all my mothers, but I'm in the process of becoming one, and it's a sweet and healing continuity that added an unexpectedly profound twist to Mother's Day this year.

I cried when the ultrasound technician told me the baby is a girl. How will I protect her? How will I accept that I can't? Each time I feel one of her kicks, already signaling her independence, I feel a blend of joy and wonder and fear and grief unlike anything I've known before. And this is what I think: maybe this child wasn't an accident after all. Maybe in a family where the love between mothers and daughters was always so unquestioned and absolute, a vacuum can't exist for long. Maybe, just maybe, when the last mother dies, a new one must be born. ❀

How will your birth as a mother be informed by the mothers before you in your lineage? Here and now capture a tale of triumph, loss, or rebirth you were told about your mother, father, or a grandparent, that you want to pass along. (Or make a list of several you want to preserve.)

Date _____

Pregnancy Log

Julie Convisser

HARBOR
In the beginning, neurons bloom like kelp.

49 DAYS
I sleep eleven hours, surface for bananas and saltines,
sleep again. We are vessel and cargo
tossed in a merciless passage of becoming.
I am seasick; I want nothing
but the pulse of this vast ocean,
a glimpse of seahorse spine.

105 DAYS
I have seen the soft mound of island,
not shore, but a place to resupply.
There are fingers and toes in my hold,
kidneys and ears. I slosh and sway,
ample with blood. The wind rises hard
in my lungs.

123 DAYS
At 1:00 and 4:00 I am awakened by an ache
I cannot name. Night's membrane
covers the stars. I navigate
without memory or compass.
What ballast weighs me, what current
do we ride?

142 Days

In ultrasonic brilliance a dolphin twists,
a cormorant shakes its wings.
Sealed inside my treasure chest:
matchstick ribs, a tiny, chambered heart.
I bear them through warm salt
to a strange continent.

156 Days

Every day now I feel the delicious turbulence
below. Flying fish: it beats
against gunwale and deck,
dives through my interior.
Hot sun, balmy wind: I have only
to keep an even keel.

173 Days

Moon pours lava over the sea.
I walk the night, unsteady in my joints.
A comet not seen for 4,000 years
arches in the northern sky.
Something as timeless, as immeasurable,
orbits in me.

196 Days

We bump and thrash forward,
list with the precious load.
Seams swell, ligaments stretch.
At dawn I taste the edge of thunder
and know we crossed
the meridian.

224 Days

Every pore chafes with salt.
We journey on and on,
through ancient waters. In my dreams
what I long for cries out
in the sweetest voice
and I take its glimmering head to my breast.

259 Days

The wind has died.
In the early spangle light
moths rise from sailcloth.
The cargo ripens as we rock.
Sand and pine tease my nostrils.
Somewhere in a new land we are expected.

285 Days

We run aground.
Everything bucks and rumbles
under the strain. Waves rush over and over
washing me to my knees.
There is only the great heaving,
the excruciating   letting go. ❦

Being pregnant, women often feel like some type of object, animal, or vessel. What do you feel like? Go as far into the image as possible. How would you like to continue to be like this emotionally and/or spiritually once your baby is born?

Date _____

Some Thoughts on Being Pregnant

Anne Lamott

I woke up with a start at 4:00 one morning and realized that I was very, very pregnant. Since I had conceived six months earlier, one might have thought that the news would have sunk in before then, and in many ways it had, but it was on that early morning in May that I first realized how severely pregnant I was. What tipped me off was that, lying on my side and needing to turn over, I found myself unable to move. My first thought was that I had had a stroke.

Nowadays I go around being aware that I am pregnant with the same constancy and lack of surprise with which I go around being aware that I have teeth. But a few times a day the information actually causes me to gasp—how on earth did I come to be in this condition? Well, I have a few suspicions. I mean, I am beginning to put two and two together. See, there was this guy. But the guy is no longer around, and my stomach is noticeably bigger every few days.

I could have had an abortion—the pressure to do so was extraordinary—and if need be, I would take to the streets, armed, to defend the right of any woman for any reason to terminate a pregnancy, but I was totally unable to do so this time psychologically, psychically, emotionally. Just totally. So I am going to have a baby pretty soon, and this has raised some mind-boggling issues.

For instance, it occurs to me over and over that I am much too self-centered, cynical, eccentric, and edgy to raise a baby, especially alone. (The baby's father was dramatically less excited than I was to find out I was pregnant, so much so that I have not seen or heard from him in months and don't expect to ever again.) At thirty-five years old,

I may be too old and too tired to be having my first child. And I really *did* think for several seconds that I might have had a stroke; it is not second nature for me to believe that everything is more or less okay. Clearly, my nerves are shot.

For example, the other day one of the innumerable deer that come down here from the mountain to eat in the garden and drink from the stream remained where it was as I got closer and closer. It was standing between me and my front door. I thought, Boy, they're getting brazen, and I walked closer and closer to it, finally to within four or five feet, when suddenly it tensed. My first thought was that it was about to lunge at me, snarling. Of course it turned instead and bolted through the woods, but I was left with the increasingly familiar sense that I am losing my grasp on reality.

One moment I'm walking along the salt marsh listening to sacred choral music on headphones, convinced that the music is being piped in through my ears, into my head, down my throat, and into my torso where the baby will be able to hear it, and the next moment I'm walking along coaching the baby on how best to grow various body parts. What are you, some kind of *nut*? I ask myself, and I know the answer is yes, *some* kind of nut, and maybe one who is not well enough to be a mother. But this is not the worst fear.

Even the three weeks of waiting for the results of the amniocentesis weren't the most fearful part, nor was the amnio itself. It was, in fact, one of the sweetest experiences of my life. My friend Manning drove me into San Francisco and stayed with me through the procedure, and, well, talk about intimate. It made sex look like a game of Twister. I lay there on the little table at the hospital with my stomach sticking out, Manning near my head holding my hands, a nurse by my feet patting me from time to time, one doctor running the ultrasound device around and around the surface of my tummy, the other doctor taking notes until it was his turn with the needles.

The ultrasound doctor was showing me the first pictures of my baby, who was at that point a four-month-old fetus. He was saying,

"Ah, there's the head now . . . there's the leg . . . there's its bottom," and I was watching it all on the screen, nodding, even though it was all just underwater photography, all quite ethereal and murky. Manning said it was like watching those first men on the moon. I pretended to be able to distinguish each section of the baby because I didn't want the doctor to think I was a lousy mother who was already judging the kid for not being photogenically distinct enough. He pointed out the vertebrae, a sweet curved strand of pearls, and then the heart, beating as visibly as a pulsar, and that was when I started to cry.

Then the other doctor took one of his needles and put it right through my stomach, near my belly button, in a circle that the ultrasound doctor had described with the end of a straw. I felt a pinch, and then mild cramping, and that was all, as the doctor began to withdraw some amniotic fluid. Now you probably think, like I thought, that this fluid is some vaguely holy saltwater, flown in from the coast for the occasion, but it is mostly baby pee, light green in color. What they do with it then is to send it to the lab, where they culture it, growing enough cells from the tissue the baby has sloughed off into the amniotic fluid to determine if there are chromosomal abnormalities and whether it is a boy or a girl, if you care to know.

During the first week of waiting, you actually believe your baby is okay, because you saw it scoot around during the ultrasound and because most babies are okay. By the middle of the second week, things are getting a bit dicey in your head, but most of the time you still think the baby is okay. But on the cusp of the second and third weeks, you come to know—not to believe but to know—that you are carrying a baby inside you in only the broadest sense of the word *baby*, because what is growing in there has a head the size of a mung bean, with almost no brain at all because all available tissue has gone into the building of a breathtaking collection of arms and knees— maybe not too many arms but knees absolutely *everywhere*.

Finally, though, the nurse who had patted my feet during the amnio called, and the first thing she said was that she had good news, and I thought I might actually throw up from sheer joy. Then she talked about the findings for a while, although I did not hear a word, and then she said, "Do you want to know its sex?" And I said yes I did.

It is a boy. His name is Sam Lamott. Samuel John Stephen Lamott. (My brothers' names are John and Steve.)

A boy. Do you know what that means? Do you know what boys have that girls don't? That's right, there you go. They have penises. And like most of my women friends, I have somewhat mixed feelings about this. Now, I don't know how to put this delicately, but I have never been quite the same since seeing a penis up close while I was on LSD years and years ago. It was an actual penis; I mean, it wasn't like I was staring at my hand for an hour and watched it turn into my grandfather's face and then into a bat and then into a penis. It was the real thing. It was my boyfriend's real thing, and what it looked like was the root of all my insanity, of a lot of my suffering and obsession. It looked like a cross between a snake and a heart.

That is a really intense thing you boys have there, and we internal Americans of the hetero persuasion have really, really conflicted feelings about external Americans because of the way you wield those things, their power over us, and especially their power over you. I ask you once again to remember the old joke in which the puzzled, defensive man says, "*I* didn't want to go to Las Vegas," then points to his crotch and says, "*He* wanted to go to Las Vegas." So it has given me pause to learn that there is a baby boy growing in my belly who apparently has all the right number of hands and feet and arms and legs and knees, a normal-size head, and a penis.

Penises are so—what is the word?—*funky*. They're wonderful, too, and I love them, but over the years such bad things have happened to me because of them. I've gotten pregnant, even when I tried so hard not to, and I've gotten diseases, where you couldn't see any evidence of disease on the man's dick and he claims not to have anything, but you end up having to get treatment and it's totally humiliating and weird, and the man's always mad at you for having caught it, even though you haven't slept with anyone else for months or even years. It is my secret belief that men love their penises so much that when they take them in to show their doctors, after their women claim to have caught a little something, the male doctors get caught up in this penis love, whack the patient (your lover) on the back, and say thunderously, "Now don't be silly, that's a *damn* fine penis you've got there."

A man told me once that all men like to look at themselves in the mirror when they're hard, and now I keep picturing Sam in twenty years, gazing at his penis in the mirror while feeling psychologically somewhere between Ivan Boesky and Mickey Mantle. I also know he will be someone who will one day pee with pride, because all men do, standing there manfully tearing bits of toilet paper to shreds with their straight and forceful sprays, carrying on as if this were one of history's great naval battles—the Battle of Midway, for instance. So of course I'm a little edgy about the whole thing, about my child having a penis instead of a nice delicate little lamb of a vagina. But even so, this is still not the worst fear.

No, the worst thing, worse even than sitting around crying about that inevitable day when my son will leave for college, worse than thinking about whether or not in the meantime to get him those hideous baby shots he probably should have but that some babies die from, worse than the fears I have when I lie awake at 3:00 in the morning (that I won't be able to make enough money and will have to live in a tenement house where the rats will bite our heads while we sleep, or that I will lose my arms in some tragic accident and will have to go to court and diaper my son using only my mouth and feet and the judge won't think I've done a good enough job and will put Sam in a foster home), worse even than the fear I feel whenever a car full of teenagers drives past my house going 200 miles an hour on our sleepy little street, worse than thinking about my son being run over by one of those drunken teenagers, or of his one day becoming one of those teenagers—worse than just about anything else is the agonizing issue of how on earth anyone can bring a child into this world knowing full well that he or she is eventually going to have to go through the seventh and eighth grades.

The seventh and eighth grades were for me, and for every single good and interesting person I've ever known, what the writers of the Bible meant when they used the words *hell* and *the pit*. Seventh and eighth grades were a place into which one descended. One descended from the relative safety and wildness and bigness one felt in sixth grade, eleven years old. Then the worm turned, and it was all over for any small feeling that one was essentially all right. One wasn't. One was no longer just some kid. One was suddenly a Diane Arbus character. It was springtime, for Hitler, and Germany.

I experienced it as being a two-year game of "The Farmer in the Dell." I hung out with the popular crowd, as jester, but boy, when those parties and dances rolled round, this cheese stood alone, watching my friends go steady and kiss, and then, like all you other cheeses, I went home and cried. There we were, all of us cheeses alone, emotionally broken by unrequited love and at the same time amped out of our minds on hormones and shame.

Seventh and eighth grades were about waiting to get picked for teams, waiting to get asked to dance, waiting to grow taller, waiting to grow breasts. They were about praying for God to grow dark hairs on my legs so I could shave them. They were about having pipe-cleaner legs. They were about violence, meanness, chaos. They were about *The Lord of the Flies*. They were about feeling completely other. But more than anything else, they were about hurt and aloneness. There is a beautiful poem by a man named Roy Fuller, which ends, "Hurt beyond hurting, never to forget," and whenever I remember those lines, which is often, I think of my father's death ten years ago this month, and I think about seventh and eighth grades.

So how on earth can I bring a child into the world, knowing that such sorrow lies ahead, that it is such a large part of what it means to be human?

I'm not sure. That's my answer: I'm not sure. One thing I do know is that I've recently been through it again, the total aloneness in the presence of almost extraterrestrially high levels of hormones. I have been thinking a lot lately of Phil Spector and his Wall of Sound, because to be pregnant is to be backed by a wall of hormones, just like during puberty, and the sense of aloneness that goes along with that is something I have been dancing as fast as I could to avoid ever having to feel again. For the last twenty-some years, I have tried everything in sometimes suicidally vast quantities—alcohol, drugs, work, food, excitement, good deeds, popularity, men, exercise, and just rampant compulsion and obsession—to avoid having to be in the same room with that sense of total aloneness. And I did pretty well, although I nearly died. But then recently that aloneness walked right into my house without knocking, sat down, and stayed a couple of weeks.

In those two weeks, tremendous amounts of support poured in, as did baby clothes and furniture. My living room started to look like a refugee relocation center, but the aloneness was here, too, and it seemed to want to be felt. I was reminded once again that the people closest to me, including my therapist, function as my pit crew, helping me to fix blown-out tires and swabbing me off between laps, and the consensus, among those individuals who make up my pit crew, was that I was probably just going to have to go ahead and feel the aloneness for a while. So I did, and I'll tell you it didn't feel very good. But somehow I was finally able to stand in that huge open wound and feel it and acknowledge it because it was real, and the fear of the pain of this wound turned out to be worse than the actual pain.

As I said, though, it didn't feel very good, and it brought me up against that horrible, hateful truth—that there wasn't anything outside myself that could heal or fill me and that everything I had been running from and searching for all my life was within. So I sat with those things for a while, and the wounds began to heal.

This all took place a few months ago, at age thirty-five. I mean, I'm old and tough and I can take it. But Sam is just a baby. Sam, in fact, hasn't even come out of the chute yet. I guess when he does, there will be all these people to help him along on his journey; he will have his pit crews, too, but at some point he will also have to start seventh grade. Maybe he will be one of those kids who get off easy, but probably not. I don't know many who did. So he will find himself at some point, maybe many times, in what feels like a crawl space, scared of unseen spiders, pulling himself along on his elbows, the skin rubbed raw, not knowing for sure whether he will ever arrive at a place where he can stand up again in the daylight. This is what it feels like to grieve a loss that is just too big, the loss of a loved one, or of one's childhood, or whatever. (And it is sometimes what it feels like to be in the middle of writing a book; and also what it feels like sometimes when you've lost your hormonal equilibrium.)

Yet we almost always come out on the other side, maybe not with all our *f-a-c-u-l-t-i-e-s* intact, as Esmé put it, but in good enough shape. I was more or less okay by ninth grade. I am more or less okay now. I really love my pit crew, and I sometimes love my work. Sometimes it feels like God has reached down and touched me, blessed me a thousand times over, and sometimes it all feels like a mean joke, like God's advisers are Muammar Qaddafi and Phyllis Schlafly.

So I am often awake these days in the hours before the dawn, full of joy, full of fear. The first birds begin to sing at quarter after five, and when Sam moves around in my stomach, kicking, it feels like there are trout inside me, leaping, and I go in and out of the aloneness, in and out of that sacred place. ❧

Describe your greatest fear regarding pregnancy, birth, or motherhood. Now describe your greatest joy. Fill in the following blanks as many times as you need to: I sometimes feel I am too _____ to have a (another) child. I sometimes feel I am not _____ enough to have a (another) child. Next, list all the wonderful qualities you know you possess that balance out your concerns. If you know the sex of your baby, what does that gender mean to you?

Date _____

Weathering Out

Rita Dove

She liked mornings the best—Thomas gone
to look for work, her coffee flushed with milk,

outside autumn trees blowsy and dripping.
Past the seventh month she couldn't see her feet

so she floated from room to room, houseshoes flapping,
navigating corners in wonder. When she leaned

against a door jamb to yawn, she disappeared entirely.

Last week they had taken a bus at dawn
to the new airdock. The hangar slid open in segments

and the zeppelin nosed forward in its silver envelope.
The men walked it out gingerly, like a poodle,

then tied it to a mast and went back inside.
Beulah felt just that large and placid, a lake;

she glistened from cocoa butter smoothed in
when Thomas returned every evening nearly

in tears. He'd lean an ear on her belly
and say: *Little fellow's really talking,*

though to her it was more the *pok-pok-pok*
of a fingernail tapping a thick cream lamp shade.

Sometimes during the night she woke and found him
asleep there and the child sleeping, too. ✤

Reflect on how your energy level or personality has shifted with pregnancy. What aspect of this difference do you hope to hold onto as a mother? Describe something your spouse, relative, or friend does for you, now that you're pregnant, that moves you—something you want to remember.

Date _____

Believe

Carla R. Du Pree

*R*ising above a situation was unspoken gospel in the Fauntroy household. So when Gaby peered out of the cab window at her family, who sat on the porch awaiting her arrival, she held strong to that belief. She pushed the door open and stepped onto the pavement. The South Bend heat pressed against her. The driver placed her bag near her feet, barely waiting for his tip as she shoved a bill into his hand. As she nudged the bag away from her swollen stomach, her family rose in unison like brown birds on the verge of flight.

It was Duchess, the mother, who descended the steps first, eyes wide with disbelief. Duchess made no effort to embrace her but exclaimed in horror, "Gabrielle, is that you?" Her sister, Dorcas, pushed past her mother, caressed Gaby's belly, then gently pulled her close. Her brother remained on the porch, looking in wonder at the dark-hued women assembled in a circle before him.

It took a moment for things to settle. Room was made on the porch for Gaby to sit. She sank into the cushioned rocker, travel-weary, and tried in vain to think of what had made her believe it'd be easier to tell them in person rather than over the telephone.

Their eyes rested on and then shifted away from Gaby's fullness. Fingers tapped against the banister. Arms folded, then unfolded. Each one of them retreated to a place on the porch to watch her from a distance. And as if they couldn't take her in all at once, they regarded her in pieces, first the full face, then the auburn hair that hung to her shoulders in a limp curl, from the wattle of her thin upper arms to the lights in her maple-colored skin. Gaby sat across from them with her eyes cast down, a hat atop her head, a rayon dress fit for travel but too

warm for the southern heat, and her legs held apart to cradle her protruding stomach.

The duchess squared her shoulders and walked away from Gaby
Everett eyed her with suspicion and wondered if her luck had run out.
A smirk on his face weighed the idea of a boyfriend who'd left her
holding the bag.

In the quiet afternoon the sun raged above them while they sat
with discontent creasing their faces, their postures as telling as the
walls they erected around them. To a stranger passing by, they were
picture perfect. Pretty people, mysterious and regal.

The duchess walked the length of the porch, then stood across
from Gaby and waited. Her fingers knotted and eased beside her. The
air was close, but she wore her usual starched blouse and black skirt.
"So you've found your way home," she said.

"I figured it was time," Gaby said, fanning herself with her hat.

"That boy John Jacob has been asking after you, but I guess you
won't be needing his attention."

Gaby couldn't answer that and didn't. She was unsure of the
duchess's stance and looked around at her siblings for a small measure
of hope. They wore their father's shape, tall and angular, but bore
their mother's fortitude. While their silence carried its own weight, the
heat roped around the porch like a noose. A pearl of sweat traveled the
length of her back, along with an uneasiness with what the weekend
would bring.

When it seemed as if Gaby could no longer bear the silence, she
excused herself. She lifted her bag, tottering as she walked, and opened
the door. And though Dorcas rose to help her, Duchess caught her by
the arm, warning her with her eyes to be still.

The screen door slammed on Gaby's back and placed her in the
center of the front hall. She took the stairs, struggling each step with
the weight of her load. When she reached the landing, something drew
her eyes downward, where Duchess stood at the foot of the stairway.
Duchess looked up and into Gaby's eyes. Neither woman spoke, and
one didn't join the other.

The duchess spun on her heels and disappeared onto the porch, headed back from where she had come.

Gaby smoothed the wrinkles in her red swing dress that she pulled from the suitcase. The brass buttons and the above-knee length were too much for Sunday service, but she could get away with the linen dress that gave her ample room to move. She rustled through her bag, pulling out clothing that needed to be hung. She had packed more than she needed, figuring if things went right she'd make it a longer stay.

Her room was small, and were it not for the chenille bedspread on the twin-sized bed it would be anchored in the past. The wallpaper that had taken hours to choose had bleached from the sun. The red flowers had faded to a somber pink, the blue background now gray.

As she draped the dresses over the crook of her arm, she looked up and found Duchess reflected in the bureau mirror. The moment she turned around, Duchess stepped into the room.

"I brought something for you, Duchess," Gaby said as she began to fish through the suitcase.

Duchess stood back and watched Gaby fumble through the disheveled arrangement of clothing. After a moment the duchess drew in a deep breath, waiting longer as Gaby searched farther into the bag.

Sweat formed on Gaby's brow and she lifted a limp wrist to her forehead to wipe it.

"Get it later," Duchess said, starting for the door.

"No, wait; I'm sure it's right here," Gaby said, looking inside the pockets and under a shelf of lingerie. Each time she came up empty.

At the point when she was convinced she had forgotten it, Duchess said again, "Get it later when you're a little more settled."

"Settled" came out hard, without warning, jolting Gaby in a way that made her catch her breath sharply. And Duchess left, cutting the warmth right out of the giving. As Gaby heard the duchess's footsteps hurrying away, she spotted a pinch of cranberry tissue in the back of her bag. She raised the small offering out of a nest of clothing. She turned it over in her hands and wondered if it would be enough, if anything would ever be enough.

⚜

It was Dorcas who pressed life into the air. She snatched Gaby by the hand and pulled her into the kitchen. "Want some sweet milk?" she said.

"Mama hasn't changed none," Gaby said behind her.

"Why are you surprised?" Dorcas said. And then, "You don't see it, do you?"

"See what?"

"Gaby, Duchess hung her faith on you."

"Don't go there, Dorcas."

Silence fell between them. Dorcas poured canned milk into a pot on the stove and added water. They were raised on warmed sweet milk. Even when the humidity was thick enough to lay on, they drank warm milk. Papa had insisted that milk protected a soul from harsh words. Dorcas handed her sister a mug filled to the brim. As she sipped from her own, she eyed Gaby carefully, enchanted with her sister's roundness and the way she held herself, like her future was a sure thing.

Growing up, Gaby had been the one who got into scrapes with the neighborhood kids. She was the one who twisted Silly Sally's arm for calling her a "wannabe," for Gaby talked proper and wore socks right below her knees.

Gaby and Duchess were clothed from the same patch. In Gaby's elementary years they fought in a fashion that left Duchess ready to lay claim that their father wouldn't have raised them at all, had she been the one who died, but would have shipped them off to their Aunt Suzie, who had raised a bunch of Fauntroy hellions. Duchess's own mother had warned her "not to worry about your young babies around near your feet, but to consider your adult children who will have you around your heart."

And so it was that long-ago summer when Gaby turned sixteen and changed the way she would live her life. They had argued over a simple thing, so simple that to this day the retelling of their story left out details of why it happened, just that it did.

On an afternoon in the early days of summer, the sun had become so unbearable that the sun-scorched grass cracked beneath their feet. The heat drove them indoors, leaving them to pace the house with little to do. Gaby and Duchess found themselves on the brink of flaring. They stood erect, their bodies clenched in cotton dresses damp against their skin. When Dorcas found them, Duchess had her palm open, ready to knock sense into her elder daughter's face. But when she raised her hand to strike her, Gaby snatched *her* by the wrist. In a small voice, Gaby had said, "Enough."

She left the room with a sense that she had won, and she knew her mother watched her stride out with a Fauntroy back and the duchess's raised chin. The next day Gaby packed her bags and left.

The memory of that moment outlived the reason for it. And now today in the kitchen, with Duchess on the porch wondering where Gaby went wrong, with paint peeling from the ceiling and windowsills cluttered with ivy, Gaby and Dorcas sat with more thoughts than words crowding the room.

Gaby sipped her milk and wished her thoughts could drown out the voices she heard on the porch, "That fool girl," she heard Duchess say. "I've tried to keep you kids from that 'nigger mess.'"

"You shouldn't worry," Dorcas said, reaching across the counter to pat Gaby's hand.

"Oh, no?"

"She'll get over it. You were the one child who left and made something of yourself, who did right by her," Dorcas said, her voice trailing off. "You know, once the baby is born, she'll be singing a different tune." And then Dorcas looked square into Gaby's face. "You could've said something to me."

"There was never the right moment, Dorcas. Each time I thought I could, the words wouldn't come."

"But aren't you afraid—to do it alone, I mean? You know what Duchess went through after Papa died. It was hard for her."

"It's not the same. I don't have to survive widowhood. Duchess had means but she had to pull her life together first," Gaby said.

"And Duchess will say, 'A woman and child leaves no room for a husband.'"

"Not necessarily. I just chose my baby first."

"She may need time with this one, Gaby."

"Well, baby sister, she's got three months."

Duchess prided herself on how she reared her children carefully. Every chance she got she supplied the local *Tribune* with Gaby's success: when she was promoted to middle management with her company, when she got preengaged to Payson Sheets (who later broke things off after steeping his presence into their lives), when she bought a brownstone in the city. Gaby's misstep unnerved her. Single mothers existed in the Fauntroys, products of divorce or relinquished loves, but not under the duchess's roof and not in her immediate family.

She carried her widowhood like armor. It became a symbol of her strength—outliving Papa—a badge of honor that required weekly visits to his grave. She wore it like a cast-iron bracelet linking her to the past, giving her reason to call up the dead any time she saw fit.

Tonight she had prepared dinner alone. She had held the potatoes under a flush of cold water, so tight her fingers cramped. The baked brisket of beef sat like a lump of worn leather in the center of her table and was horrible to cut. Once the napkins were placed and the candles lit, in celebration of Gaby's homecoming, the family bowed their heads and formed a ring with their hands. It was the closest Gaby and Duchess had come to touching that day.

Everett said grace. "Lord, make us true and thankful, indeed, for the food—um, and baby, we're about to receive. . . ."

As he blessed their dinner, Gaby glanced across the table at her mother, whose eyes narrowed and then embraced her with scorn. The evening sun would set on Duchess working a way to steal the words from her neighbors' lips which she knew were bound to fall.

Quietly Gaby shifted in her seat as the baby stirred within her. Never before in her life had she so worn her mother's shame.

⁂

On the edge of morning Gaby stood in the kitchen, pushing her gift from home toward the duchess's hands, which were covered with flour. Gaby had taken much effort to find a dove-shaped crystal.

Duchess held the gift in her palm, then slowly disengaged the wrapping. For a moment Gaby thought the sight of the lone bird cast in cranberry would soften Duchess's face. But the duchess gave it a once-over glance and placed it on the counter beside the canister of flour.

She had been kneading a mound of dough when Gaby first entered and continued to do so as Gaby stood at her back. The set of her erect shoulders motioned forward as the duchess leaned into the spongy heap. "Cynthia Early got engaged this past week and expects a spring wedding next year. You remember her, don't you?"

Yes, Gaby remembered Cynthia Early. Cynthia managed to do everything before Gaby. She was early to graduate from college, early to land a job, to get a promotion, to lay herself down to the first man asking, and equally as early to claim otherwise. But the duchess heard the good.

"Oh, is she?" Gaby said. "Well, good for her."

"And do you know *who* she's going to marry?"

"No, I don't, Duchess." And to herself, *But I'm sure you'll tell me.*

"Why, Payson Sheets. He owns several stores now since you two were last together. Doing quite fine for himself these days. Yes, indeed. And to think he could've been my son-in-law."

Gaby pulled out an apple from a bowl on the table. She bit down hard and savored the sweet white flesh that crunched inside her mouth. She ate it down to its core without saying another word. She tore off a paper towel from its spool and wiped her hands.

"You hadn't planned on going to church, had you?" Duchess said, her back still turned, leaning the heels of her hands farther into the dough.

"As a matter of fact, I had," Gaby said.

"I would prefer if you stayed home."

"Duchess."

"Your papa would want you to stay put," Duchess said, turning to face Gaby, and as she did her floured hand swung out, pushing the glass bird over the edge.

They both looked down at the fallen bird, which landed at the duchess's feet. Duchess's hands fluttered to her face, then dropped, white and soiled, to her thighs. She stepped over the bird toward Gaby. Instead of the comfort Gaby expected, Duchess brushed past her with hands that whitened her skirt, pushing the black near a muted gray.

Gaby lifted her nightgown as a dry wind lurched through her open window. Unlike anything she'd ever felt, the heat took to South Bend with a passion. With it came a heaviness that weighted her skin. With a child on the way it seemed even more brutal. She drifted in and out of sleep, shifting her body to reach the right valley in the mattress. It was old—everything about this house was old and noted for an unclaimed past, from the winter green awning along the southern porch to the furniture cluttering all three floors. Most of the furniture was purchased from secondhand shops. Old things were reliable, Duchess had said. Old things dragged their history with them, Gaby thought.

Despite the clutter, as a child Gaby learned to move through darkness, making a game of seeing how far she could go without turning on the lights. Duchess frequently scolded her but Gaby had taken to the night, had learned the feeling of closed space and the lightness of an open room. Her brother and sister would never see to a banging shutter in the middle of the night. Gaby didn't mind, though; the darkness made things bigger than they were, so daylight brought convenience.

She rose to lift the window farther on its hinge, then peeled her gown away from her body. She crept downstairs to the kitchen for water, opened the back door, and stepped onto the porch. She looked up at the maidenhair ferns and spider plants that hung from the ceiling and swayed in the breeze. A floral scent wafted from the garden and reached Gaby's nose in gentle bursts. Weeping willows combed their branches along the awning, and the night blooms of moon plants stood stark white against the blanket darkness.

She thrust her weight to and fro on the glider. As she did, the kitchen light came on. Duchess pushed herself onto the porch. A heaviness came with her entry. "I figured it was you out here stirring up the night," she said, pulling the air away.

"It's this heat."

"A little thing like the heat shouldn't bother you none. Thirty South Bend summers can make you get used to anything. Seems like the only way I can tell it's here is by looking at my flowers. My dragon lilies start to wilt. Water can't help them, and the shade is the devil in disguise.

"Well, I'm going to head back to bed. Get you some rest," she said, moving toward the door.

Gaby called out after her, "Mama, we should talk," but the words were lost as the screen door slammed into place.

In the doorway Duchess paused. Gaby held her breath, hoping she had heard after all. She wished her mother would come sit beside her like they used to sit, with their hands touching in the dark.

Gaby heard Duchess turn to switch off the light and start for the stairs. The farther her mother stepped away, the easier it became to breathe. The lightness of air surrounded her.

But the duchess hadn't stepped away. She emerged from the darkness of the house to the porch, careful not to misstep. She swept across the landing to the railing, where she stood with her chin lifted to the moon, whose blue light splintered through the shaded trees and marked her face gray.

Gaby waited until her eyes adjusted to the shadow of her mother before she said, "It'll be your first grandchild, Duchess." There, the words escaped before she could breathe them in again.

"I would have preferred a first son-in-law."

"The baby's due this fall."

"That's just what you need, a temperamental child."

"I keep craving boiled peanuts."

"*Hmh*, peanuts will make you fat for sure. I remember when I was pregnant with you I couldn't get enough of raisins. I swore I'd never so much as eat a grape after I had you."

"Did you like being pregnant, Mama?"

Duchess paused before she said, "I guess I did. My skin stayed clear. My hair was so thick I had to wear it in a French braid, and my nails—my nails were splendid." Her voice trailed off as she looked down at her splayed hands, remembering. "But that was years ago and times were different. Your daddy took good care of me. I didn't so much as want for a glass of water, he was right there tending to my every need.

"I keep wanting to ask you what is it, this thing you've done?"

Gaby watched Duchess clench her hands.

"I've got it all worked out, Duchess," she said. Then, after a moment, "You don't understand, do you? I planned this pregnancy. It wasn't a mistake."

"Then you're a bigger fool than I imagined. What smart girl throws away her life on an idea that she can handle another? What if your baby is sickly or you can't find someone to care for him?"

"My friends will help."

"Friends aren't family," Duchess said, snapping back the air.

She bristled, and the starchiness of her night clothes sounded out her movement from the porch steps to the door. As she reached for the handle, Gaby said, "I think it's a girl, Duchess."

"You're carrying too high. Your hips are as wide as a Hottentot's and your back is too broad. It's a boy."

The door opened, yawning until it reached its frame, and the words hung in the air, weighted like magnets to the evening sky. And in the stillness of the night, Gaby sat measuring what she had heard. A thin smile spread across her lips. The willow's leaves rustled, and a breeze blew in that stayed with her till morning.

The next day Gaby rose from sleep and made her way to the third floor porch. Peeking through the trees' foliage had been a childhood treat— watching neighbors leave and return home from work with no wear on their minds at all of who could see them make public their private acts. On occasion she caught Julie Birk's boyfriend slipping out of her house. Gaby knew when Mr. Stokes pulled into the drive across the way, Mrs. Stokes appeared on the lawn.

But today as Gaby breathed in the faint scent of morning, she spotted a woman in black striding purposefully along the sidewalk, a spectacle of grace. It was the duchess returning home from Sunday service. Her gait was unusually spry. She touched the ribboned heads of youngsters playing on the sidewalk as she hurried past them. Now and then she reached up to press the flat of her sprawling hat down on her head. Her Bible remained tucked beneath one arm as she waved to a neighbor, who sat on his porch reading the morning paper.

Gaby imagined the duchess at her usual station at Mt. Zion, the aisle seat in the front left pew, with her hymnbook open in the cradle of her hand. With the first note sung, Duchess stole away from life's circumstances. And when Reverend Lee's words struck a chord that mirrored her life, she raised a gloved hand, a testament that she understood what life had wrought her. Gaby imagined her reading scripture with parted lips, wiping dry her watering eyes, while she looked around, making sure no one saw them.

A yard from home, Duchess stepped down from the curb, and rather than look for oncoming traffic she leaned back toward the open sky. As she did, a solid wind caught her full face, lifting her hat off her head before sailing it toward the street. Before it flew completely out of reach, she lunged forward and caught it like a bird between gloved hands.

But what threw Gaby the most was the way Duchess's face broke into a smile, not broad and wondrous, but a giving smile that's born from a stirring in the heart. Gaby pulled her robe tighter and hurried downstairs to the back of the house. She wanted to greet Duchess with flowers, so she stumbled through the brush in her bare feet, looking for roses that didn't bow at the stem but looked toward the sun, like Gaby, pressing their faith against the very thing that could harm them. ❀

Record what you know about your mother's pregnancies and/or those of other women relatives. How has being pregnant changed your relationship to your mother? How has it solidified what already exists between you? Describe anything surprising your mother has done or said during your pregnancy.

Date _____

1963 Creation

Lake Boggan

*T*hen we fell asleep
   at an age when sleep came easily
the seed of you, planted, would burrow into me
somehow in that night in the green house
not far from the yellow house
where I had been born.
Dogs slumbered on the floor
while my body transformed.
Why didn't my system spark
or quiver with electrical impulses
that ignite when life arcs?
How could I sleep while your cells divided
like bubbles in a rich broth?

I did become giddy after that night,
hungry, God I was hungry.
I needed grapefruit and ice cubes,
whole fryers and ice cream.
With hunger came self-desire.
I was inseparable from the mirror,
stood naked most often, balanced
between trance and rapture
knowing I was rooted with child.

Honestly, it was a selfish time,
it all happened to me alone;
like a whale offshore,
it must be there
but my eyes saw only me.
I stared into the distance
I walked alone over my flesh.

I'm sorry but even the milk
belonged to me; the hunger
and staring at myself,
believing I could smell and hear and see ghosts.
I was rocked independent of the world
and the swaying within.
I was visible only to myself
in those days and I felt things
I couldn't share as if I might
at any moment, be taken away
like a missile aimed at Cuba.

Everyone in my family
would sit on the edge of their beds
and listen to the news. ❦

In what ways is your pregnancy a selfish time for you and/or a private time for you? In what ways do you feel "independent of the world"? If entering the state of timelessness has changed you, consider how.

Date _____

Dancing with the Paper Rose

Suzy Vitello

Twelve years ago, when I still swam through the blue cheese dressing of my salad days, I blithely began my first family. I was twenty-five, and carried like a pesky cyst a childhood memory of one husband's *The Newlywed Game* response to the question, "The age at which a woman's body is most attractive." The answer, of course, had been twenty-five.

The figure that glared at me from the mirror in our modest home in Chandler, Arizona, revealed differently. At five months I'd already gained the twenty-eight pounds I was allowed. I could not keep food out of my mouth that first time. My job as a dietary technician for Good Samaritan Hospital didn't help. Calories were a fingertip away eight hours a day. Nausea easily assuaged by yet another raisin-toast-and-cream-cheese sandwich. I wasn't alone, however. Even greater than misery's yearning for company, is that of a large pregnant woman, and, thankfully, I was surrounded by corpulent primiparas.

My coworkers, all in their twenties, were challenging the seams of their orange and black tunics in similar fashion. We were, the lot of us, sassy young mothers-to-be, who felt a sudden hormonally induced hubris toward our infirm charges: patients who refused, day after day, to fill out their menus in a timely fashion.

"Sorry, time's up!" the renal diet technician would scold, whipping the watermarked menu from the tray of a patient dying of kidney failure, "Looks like low-protein toast and vanilla Ensure again tomorrow, Mrs. Wallateen."

We suddenly didn't have time for anyone's shit. Imagine our supervisor, fending off the reams of complaints against us, and our collective petulant response, "Our ankles are soooo swollen, we can't just stand there and stand there."

We were like a cult, spending our breaks stuffing our faces with comfort food from the cafeteria, comparing stretch marks, ideas on names, anecdotes about our loving, though completely stupid, husbands. Half of us were planning on nursing, the other half pilfering Enfamil and Similac from the maternity ward. Occasionally, *very* occasionally, a couple of us would take a sobering elevator ride up to the NICU (Neonatal Intensive Care Unit) and stare behind the thick glass at two-pound yellow preemies, squirming amid the Frankenstein wires secured to them with patches of adhesive.

There were poems and essays Scotch-taped to the window, some attached to Polaroids of hopelessly tiny infants, miracle babies who might forever be blind, palsied, or respirator dependent. And the stories about the ones who didn't make it; like roadside crucifixes, these testimonies of familial love tore into me.

I performed calculations on my own pregnancy each time I visited the NICU: twenty-five weeks; just over a pound, 20 percent chance of survival. Twenty-eight weeks, almost three pounds, 60 percent. Thirty-two weeks had my baby in one of the less dire incubators; my child would be one of the bigger, less-damaged preemies in the unit. I began to relax a little toward the beginning of my thirty-eighth week. I would not have a premature baby, but the horrific unknown still lay between me and my bundle of joy; the thousands of things that can go wrong during delivery. At Good Samaritan, a paper rose was taped outside the door of a woman whose baby had not survived: a subtle indicator to the staff to turn off the usual postpartum shtick in favor of sympathy and respect. Diet techs were not allowed in these rooms.

My baby was due on Christmas Day. My husband, Frank, had trucked up to the hinterlands in search of a festive cedar. The one he brought home and erected in our living room competed with, but did not exceed, my own girth. Somewhere in a bottom drawer there is a videotape that proves this. The same tape features an enormous young woman on Christmas Day, sitting cross-legged on the floor, popping chocolates into her mouth, staring blankly at the unopened gifts for her unborn child.

I am now thirty-seven years old and pregnant with my third child. At middle age, I am engaged in the great fight with gravity, reading up on the challenge of parenting teenagers, and juggling my OB visits amidst soccer practices and PTA meetings. I have on my nightstand, *Reviving Ophelia* and *What to Expect When You're Expecting*. I am alternately tickled with the prospect of tiny socks, talcum, and tender behinds, and repelled by the sheer enormity of the psychic, emotional, and physical energy required to usher a little one from conception through kindergarten, but I am well aware that many of my contemporaries have not had the luxury of bemoaning successful pregnancies. I haven't forgotten the paper rose.

Like so many others my age, I have had the paradoxical experience of skin that grows thinner with every media event, and a heart that hardens in response. Now that I no longer work in a hospital, do not have the advantage of a NICU in my daily life, I look for more subtle forms of emotional manipulation. When I was twenty-five, I had horrible nightmares throughout my entire pregnancy, chock full o' serpents, chasms, and dark water. At thirty-seven I am again experiencing bad dreams. A week ago I dreamed I was awaiting the results of my prenatal AFP test. When they arrived, they were in the form of columns and columns of cryptic numbers under category headings like DNA, digestion, experimental surgery. The values were not explained, and I had phoned the doctor for help, but when the doctor called back, I'd misplaced the test results. The nightmare-aspect of this dream did not involve the results themselves, but the frustration of trying to find this missing document that seemed to have vanished into thin air. I have had numerous of these dreams: the inability to find or dial the correct phone number or locate the necessary items called for in a recipe. Losing my airline ticket during final boarding.

If there's one thing that's becoming clearer and clearer to me as my belly takes on the familiar globe shape, it's that I don't know a thing. That *Titanic*'s heartthrob Leo what's-his-name's euphoric claim of being "King of the World" is as fleeting as a baby's first smile. For a split second you've got all your balls in the air, all burners going, completely in charge, and *bam*, as my friend Tom Spanbauer says, "You're going this way, and then shit happens, and then you're going that way."

Being pregnant, as it turns out, is not about keeping in, but instead, it is the first step in letting go. Allowing a part of myself to cleave into something completely its own, and having the grace to attend this miracle of life while respecting the whole person that I continue to be.

I still pause in front of the mirror from time to time, knowing sadly that thirty-seven would never be an answer to any query on the cosmetic value of women's bodies, pregnant or not. As I glance over the enormous areolas, the distended navel, and the superhighway of veins that claim my body, there is, at times, a little voice distilled from the clamoring buzz of superfluous information I've taken in over the years; a voice that quiets me with its offbeat wisdom, sneering, almost, as it says, "Yo, Mama, what makes you think this is about you?"

What is your style of handling "the odds" while pregnant? Will this be how you hope to teach your child to deal with possibilities? How is your view of your age affecting your pregnancy and feelings about mothering? If you've had any night-mares or daymares, describe them. How can they be used to help you; what messages do they hold for you?

Date _____

Ants

Bonni Goldberg

*E*llen stands in the middle of my new living room. Her eleven-month-old baby, Jesse, is pointing to the parquet.

"Floor," says Ellen and turns to admire the view.

Jesse frowns. So I ease myself down to get a closer look.

"Ant." I pronounce it like a teacher.

"Zay, it's fantastic," Ellen says to me.

It *is* a wonderful house. We are lucky to have found it when we did: before the baby was born, before I was too big to deal with a move, past the first trimester's gripping nausea, and after the amnio came out OK so I could finally breathe a sigh of relief. In fact, the timing was reassuring—a sign that Oregon was the right choice, for all of us.

The ant is gone, and now Jesse is chewing on a rattle shaped like an ice-cream cone.

"Come on, Jesse and I will take you to lunch."

When we sit on the floor to put on our shoes, we see three more ants crawling on the wall. Ellen squashes them like pushing buttons on the phone.

I get home in time to nap before starting dinner. I'm still in the dreamy state of a satisfying indulgence. So far the best part of pregnancy is eating all the foods I'd given up for the sake of Joe's low-fat diet. Today, I ordered, and polished off, a plate of fettuccine Alfredo.

As I drift off I hear jays outside the bedroom window: better jays and ants than the pigeons and waterbugs back in Philly.

I wake up to the phone ringing. It's Joe. I spare him the details of what I eat when he isn't around. Actually, I'm sparing myself; he rolls his eyes at dinner whenever I put butter and sour cream on my potato or heap guacamole on a burrito. He says he's just impressed by all that I can put away, but I think that he's a little jealous. If he hadn't been right there in the OB's office, he never would have believed that my doctor wants me to gain extra weight. Despite my hearty appetite, I'm at the low end of the charts that track a normal pregnancy. People often comment on how small I am. Not people, women. They say things like: "you look great, hardly showing at all, I blew up like a balloon." It bothers me, worries me, actually. I understand the subtext: you're supposed to be big; it means a healthy baby.

The doctor says the baby is okay, but that it's better to have the statistics on our side. The more on our side the better, I say.

Joe tries to reassure me. "You look plenty big to me, Zay. Big and beautiful," he says every night as I get out of the tub and he hands me a towel.

Tonight I wake at 2:30 A.M. Quietly, I go to the kitchen. I'm getting used to middle-of-the-night waking, which started about two weeks ago. Ellen says its preparation for when the baby will need night feedings. Since she's my only Portland friend who already has a child, I take her word for it, and maybe the baby is already hungry.

When I flip on the lights, the countertop looks wavy. First I think my eyes are adjusting, until I get closer to the bowl of bananas. I freeze. A surge of heat rises up my neck, and a stale wave of nausea follows right behind. I shudder. They practically cover the counter and half the bananas. My first thought is to wake Joe, let him take care of it. But they're only ants for god sakes, and I'm a grown woman, almost a mother.

I can't bring myself to kill them: too many and too much carnage. I go for the roll of paper towel, tear off two long sheets and dampen them. My bare feet feel tender on the tile floor. With one wad I wipe the ants away and into the other towel. I take them to the front door and shove the towel under the hedges. I've seen Joe do a similar thing with spiders. He has a spider tattoo on his leg. The night air is damp and smells like earth. I take long, deep breaths.

My stomach settles. I haven't had that feeling in quite a while. It reminds me of those weeks right after we moved cross-country. I felt so alone, sick to my stomach in a strange apartment while Joe was establishing himself at the new branch office. I spent more time with the realtor than with my husband.

In the kitchen there are still ants on the counter. Where are they coming from? I crouch down on the floor and spot the trail. I drag more paper towel along the edge of the baseboards from the kitchen to the front hall and out the door, wash my hands twice, then head back to bed. The back of my neck tingles. I grab at the spot cringing. But it's only a fine strand of my hair. I burrow into the covers and sleep.

"Call an exterminator," Joe offers over breakfast.

"Of course," I say. But what I want is admiration or thanks for not waking him, maybe some sympathy.

"How big?" The woman asks.

"Regular size, I guess."

"Sugar ants. Starts every May. Such a mild, wet winter brings them early. I can send the boss with some poison today around four."

"No, I'm pregnant!" It just comes out.

"Oh, congratulations. Your first?"

"Yes." I'm embarrassed. "Is there some other way to keep them out of the house?"

"Well, I've heard of sprinkling cayenne pepper across the front door," she says. "It's supposed to break the scent of the trail, or maybe they don't cross over it because of how it feels. I don't remember, just don't tell the boss it was me that told you. Good luck."

I feel much better. I'm pretty sure there's cayenne on the spice shelf. From the kitchen window, it looks like there'll be a break in the rain. It isn't really the chance of poison reaching the baby, it's intentionally killing anything while pregnant. This is bigger magic than Joe's tattoo. I potted twice the usual number of bulbs this winter, and I took such extra special care with them that Joe said it bordered on devotion. But ants have to go, before they make their way into the nursery and the rest of the house. They get the outside, we get the inside—that's fair. When I find the cayenne, I check on the amaryllis. They are the same color. I pour a thick line across the outside of the front door and another just inside the foyer. I phone Joe at the office and leave him a message about it before leaving to do the shopping.

As I roll my cart down the aisles, people smile at me. It isn't really me they're grinning at; it's the baby. It happens everywhere now. I always smile back because I'm the baby's link to more than just my extra weight.

Leaving the heavier bags in the car for Joe to bring in later, I'm careful to step over the cayenne on both sides of the entrance. It's raining again, and I don't want to track the pepper into the house. No ants in sight, I put away the groceries, make myself a sandwich, and phone Ellen. We're meeting this afternoon to make a list of what I need to buy to be ready for the baby. She speaks fondly about when she was expecting and went to lunch and shopped for baby things with her other pregnant friends. But I like being the only pregnant woman I know in town. It makes my altered state feel more special.

"Maybe we should hang crossbones over the doorway, too," Joe is joking, of course. But I don't think it's funny, and I might have said something, except that he's already picked up the baby list from the hall table and I'm more interested in his reaction. It overwhelms me.

"We can get started this weekend," he kisses me gently on the lips.

At 2 A.M., I get out of bed to pee. I stand in front of the bathroom mirror for a while looking at my belly and going over what I remember of the baby list in my head. I'm trying to mentally prepare the route we'll drive today to get as much done as efficiently as possible. Weekends are precious time together.

I wake up at 5:30 A.M.; too soon to disturb Joe. I hear robins. Their song makes me want waffles. There's a faint, pale light filtering through the kitchen window. The sky looks so still I don't want to breathe too hard. When I tiptoe toward the fridge I see the black mass pooling, glistening, spreading over my counter and teeming from the saucer where the honey jar sits; my throat closes up. Invasion. For a moment I leave my body, and the baby with it, and when I return, I'm dizzy and shaking. Why is this happening? I can't let this happen. I pull off both slippers and start slapping the countertop. I'm screaming.

I'm screaming, "I warned you dammit." I'm screaming, "You have the whole frigging yard, the whole rest of the world. Get out!" I tell them, "Leave us alone or I'll smash every single one of you." I tell them, "I'll do it. I will. This is my house, my food, my baby."

There are tears in my eyes so I can't really see, but I know where the trail is and I go down on my knees to pound at it too. That's where Joe finds me.

"My god, Zay, what's wrong?"

When I can't respond, can't stop, he moves in closer, crouches down and embraces me as he reaches for the slippers. The touch of his warm body makes me let go of them and rock back sobbing. After a while we both stand up. The counter is strewn with ant carcasses. I look at them, then at Joe. He's waiting to see what I do. I'm sure he's afraid of me now. The baby is flip-flopping inside me like it wants out. I cross my arms over my belly and throw up into the sink.

Joe doesn't even try to change my mind. He only offers to drive me to Nature's Bounty. But I want to go alone. So he puts away the Yellow Pages without calling a single exterminator and starts on the laundry.

I return with something called Orange Shield. It's in an opaque spray bottle and the label says "natural repellent." The man at Nature's says it works great; it's a product they use at the store. I'm still shaken by my outburst. Joe was so understanding, but I don't understand. I'm scared, not only of the fury that overcame me, but for the baby. What had I done? I'm supposed to keep this baby safe inside me and not only can't I feed it enough, now who knows what damage I've done? I'll use this natural thing, that the ants don't like, to steer them away. When I get home I spray the threshold generously and do it throughout the day and before we go to bed. It makes the foyer smell like orange peels. It is a clean and lovely smell.

We agree that if I wake in the middle of the night I'll rouse Joe. But I sleep until morning and the kitchen and foyer are free and clear all day. I only spray twice on Sunday, and Monday morning there are still no ants.

And we decide to get started on the baby list next weekend. I eat a hearty and leisurely breakfast of waffles, eggs, yogurt, and the pregnancy tea I'd also bought at Nature's. I'm going to observe a prenatal yoga class at Ellen's health club and then to my OB for a weight check. I put on my favorite black knit maternity pants and a royal blue tunic.

When I get into the car, I notice the brochure on the passenger seat: *The Story Behind Orange Shield*. It must have come with the bottle and slipped out of the bag. I stuff it into my purse and finish fiddling with the seat belt, which is getting more difficult to adjust over my belly.

In the health club I'm taken to a small booth beside the classroom to watch. I love the yoga class. The instructor's matte voice comes through a speaker hanging from the ceiling. Two rows of pregnant women stand in profile, shift into poses called Half-Moon, Mountain, Warrior, Goddess. I can't wait to join them; their big bellies and outstretched arms remind me of the procession of great bears on an ancient Greek vase I once saw at a museum in Philly. During the relaxation portion at the end, I close my eyes and feel my whole body ease as I follow along with the visualization enfolding myself and my baby in white light and rocking us both gently, effortlessly.

At the doctor's, I don't want to disturb my state with glossy magazine articles about pregnancy. I pull out the Orange Shield brochure. It explains that ants don't just dislike the odor, the oil in orange essence suffocates them by clogging their respiratory system. Of course they hate the smell. At least it's safer for baby than the exterminator's poison each spring. I pick up a magazine after all, and I sit in the waiting room until it's my turn. ❀

Reflect on your current feelings of territoriality and your ability to control people, places, and things. Relate your thoughts to parenting.

Date _____

Pregnant Poets Swim Lake Tarleton, New Hampshire

Barbara Ras *(For Emily Wheeler)*

You dive in, head for the other side, sure
that to swim a lake means to cross it,
whole. I am slow to follow,
repelled by edgewater rife with growth, the darker
suck of the deep. You lead,
letting go so surely you possess. I surrender.
Midlake we rest, breathless, let up our feet.
Our bellies are eight-month fruits
fabulous with weightlessness.
We have entered summer like a state of pasture,
pregnancy like a state of mind so full
nothing else can be.
Sharing this is simple: the surprise of a tomato
still perfect after days in a pocket.
Brown lines began in pubic hair, arced
up abdomens to our navels.
Here is the circle made flesh.
How much water does it take to make blood?
Where do Tibetans get the conches
they blow to release the trapped sound of the sea?
Our talk slows to the lengthening loop of the blood,
pauses for tiny hands, tiny feet to beat their sayso.
"Marianne" lasts as long as a complete sentence
before the next utterance floats up, "Moore."
We are the gardens. We are the toads.

The season of wetness is upon us.
Leap. Leap for all the kingdoms
and all the waters,
the water that breaks,
the rain, the juice, the tide,
the dark water that draws light down to life. ❦

How does your relationship to your pregnancy differ from other women you know who are pregnant? Without judging your style of being pregnant, how do you feel it reflects on your future style of mothering?

Date _____

Infertile Friends

Jen Karetnik

*T*he toughest moments in my pregnancy were not when, in my first trimester, my hepatitis B test came back "equivocal" and had to be repeated. After an agonizing four days, I was eventually found negative.

They were not when, the day before Christmas, protein tests predicted that my baby had a one-in-ten chance of having a chromosomal disorder "incompatible with life." They were also not during amniocentesis, performed on New Year's Eve day, when the needle sipping up amniotic fluid like a starving hummingbird disturbed the fetus so much her arm-buds started to wave in panic.

The hardest times were not in my sixth month, when I became allergic to shellfish, yogurt, and MSG, and suffered episode after episode of violent and dangerous vomiting before I figured out why. Not when I began to show and my boss suddenly became so dissatisfied with my "performance" that he threatened to fire me. They were not in my eighth month, when infectious bacteria were found in my birth canal. Nor were they when my water broke a week early, leaving me a desk full of work to finish when I came home from the hospital.

No, the most difficult instance of my pregnancy transpired when I went into labor on the erstwhile due date of a close friend who had lost her first baby early on in the pregnancy. A child Ann had been wanting and planning for all the years I've known her: long, long before I thought about becoming a mother myself.

In the first weeks of my pregnancy, I'd called to tell Ann, only to find out that she'd just miscarried (I didn't know she was pregnant).

I held my tongue—and my abdomen—instead. I knew there would never be a good time to impart my news, but I couldn't cause her any more pain just then.

Eventually, though, I had to let her know. Ann took it with better grace than I thought she would. She said she'd been depressed, but she and her husband were ready to try again. She sounded positively chipper.

I should have known better. Infertility is so much more complicated, on every level, than simple competitiveness. Of course Ann was happy for me. But a problem *did* exist. She was stressed out and miserable, especially as months went by and she didn't conceive, and I didn't hear from her.

Nor could she bear to visit with me. On a visit to Miami, Ann eventually phoned to arrange a lunch date. Then she called back to cancel. Minutes later, she reinstated the engagement. And changed her mind. "I really do want to see you," she insisted. "But I just can't."

Finally, and to my everlasting shame, I lost my temper. "Do what you need to do," I told her. "Just make a decision." I hung up, crying.

In hindsight—and my own defense—I have to admit I wasn't too emotionally stable myself. I was eight months along at the time, and had had a lousy week arguing with my boss. I'd reached the point in the pregnancy where people were treating my belly as a handicap. To me, her dilemma felt like rejection. She wasn't being a good friend.

But I knew, even at the time, that my attitude was not very supportive. Wasn't I the one who had too much to drink and went on a crying jag when I learned a friend of mine was pregnant with her second baby before I'd even conceived my first?

Still, the difference between sympathy and empathy is, in the end, a baby. And after a year of temporary "infertility" (we're so quick with this label these days) and a trying pregnancy, I gave birth to a beautiful baby girl. Not on Ann's due date, thankfully, but the day after.

Ann and I did eventually make up. I was grateful our friendship hadn't been sacrificed to my insensitivity. And we ultimately saw each other after my daughter was born. But I didn't insist she meet Zoe, especially since she'd just miscarried for a second time. I learned not to force the issue. Confronting an infertile friend with proof of your own fertility isn't very perceptive. In friendship—as well as in motherhood—caring is often about taking those difficult moments on yourself. ❧

Has your sense of what caring means shifted since you've been pregnant? Reflect on how your pregnancy has affected your friendships. Do any of these changes seem like preparation for mothering your baby?

Date _____

Bastille

Rachael A. Silverman

*T*he night I find out I am pregnant, I am closing the drop-in center alone. I offer to stay late because the receptionist finally has a date with this guy she has been after ever since I started working at the Cleveland People's Clinic, about six months ago. This is the first job I have had in a while that I like.

The other reason I stay is because I want to be alone when I take my pregnancy test. I can take the test here for free, because the regular health clinic is in the same building as the mental health clinic. All the girls who work here run a test on themselves every time they are five minutes late. But I am a lot more than five minutes late, I am four weeks late. Plus I don't feel so good. So of course I am not too surprised when the test is positive. I am only surprised at how calm I feel.

I do take this moment to go through what I call the Checklist of My Life. I started the checklist the time I was sixteen and decided to drive cross-country with my boyfriend who had just graduated from high school. When he left me in Rapid City and I had to call my parents for a bus ticket home, I had lots of time for reflection.

At this point the list looks like this:

age: 24

marital status: no prospects

employment: low-paid mental health worker

education: community college

physical health: good

mental health: just fine

Now I have one more item to add:

pregnancies: one

The test is just a long piece of white plastic with a pink plus sign on the end. It feels like the kind of flimsy toy that comes in sugar cereal boxes. I put the positive test in a plastic sandwich bag, put the bag in my pocket, lock the door, and ride my bike home. When I get there, I put my arms around my Bastille's muscular neck and tell him there is going to be a baby. Bastille licks my face with his soft loose tongue.

Bastille is forty pounds of solid black dog, but when he came to me a couple of years ago he was a skinny puppy. I had just started my last job working at a treatment center, in the same neighborhood as the clinic I work at now, when I heard the sound of crying outside. I opened the door and there he was, yelping and straining against the rope two clients had used to tie him to the wooden porch railings. They were off-and-on homeless, this couple, and sometimes lived in a downtown single-room apartment. The woman, Maggie, was crying as her husband Paul was looking at me and saying, "Now sweetheart, you know we can't keep him. Jane will take him, won't you now?"

"I'll make sure he gets a home," I answered, as Maggie sobbed against Paul's shoulder. "Does he have a name?"

"We call him Nugget," said Paul. And then they left, walking slowly down the street, I think maybe a little drunk.

I bent down to pet the dog. He was wearing a pink and blue plastic rosary and had a piece of rope for a collar. He wiggled around and licked my arm several times, nudged his wet nose in my hand, and that was all it took for me to fall in love. I went home and checked with my landlord, who said I could keep him, but if he did any damage to the house I would have to pay for it. I called him Nugget for a couple of days. "Nugget, come," and "Nugget, no," but it was a lousy name and I felt stupid using it. So I named him Bastille, which seemed like a better fit for a dog who appeared to have his own ideas about how things should go. I put his rosary away in a drawer, took him for his shots, and welcomed him to my life.

Bastille could get out of anything, could do whatever was necessary to free himself. He found every way possible out of my backyard; he would climb or tunnel or even temporarily dissolve his bones. But I would always get him back. Someone would call, "Hey, I think I saw your dog running around the Big Bear parking lot," or, "I found your dog, he's in my backyard." Whenever I picked him up, he could barely manage to act contrite. He would only slink down low to the ground and avoid my eyes for a couple of minutes. Then he would be his own happy self again.

Once, when I am at work, Bastille gets out of the yard and ends up at a pro-hemp meeting. He is out for about an hour, and the guy in charge leaves me two messages on my machine before I am able to get there. The first message is very mellow. "Hey, it's Steve. I got your dog. Why don't you swing by my meeting at the Peaceful Pear and pick him up? Peace for all." The second message, twenty-five minutes later, is more urgent: "Please come by and get your dog *now*." In the background of the message I can hear Bastille's high-pitched yelp. The Peaceful Pear is some kind of art gallery, and when I get there, Bastille is running around in little circles, blocked in a corner by a couple of large paintings leaning on chairs.

I try almost every form of discipline, applied consistently for weeks at a time. Praising him for coming back, hitting him for disobeying, throwing water on his head for jumping on everyone at my front door. It is amazing that nothing ever worked.

Despite all this, Bastille is the only member of the male sex, besides my dad, that I count on. At night we cuddle on the couch, and after work we take long walks through the neighborhood or go to Highground Park. But what I love most is taking him to the beach at

Lake Erie. He will chase birds and waves for hours, running back and forth on shore until he is a little black dot. If there is a storm traveling across the lake, he will sit on the sand and stare at the lightning moving from the water to the sky, until his fur stands up and quivers with electricity.

People walking the beach always stop and stare at him. Do you see that dog? they ask each other. He is faster and more graceful than any other animal I have ever seen. On the lake he is not a penned up city dog, but the elemental dog. Anyone can see that the wild in him deserves complete respect.

After I tell Bastille about the baby, I let him out for a few minutes. Then I call my boyfriend Neal, also the baby's father.

"What's up?" I ask. "What're you doing?"

"Not much. I'm going out to see some bands. You want to come?"

"No thanks, I'm pretty wiped." And I understand at that moment that I am on my own. Neal is always happy to have me tag along, but that is as far as it goes. I say goodbye and hang up.

The next day I phone my sister and my parents, who live on the West Side, and tell them. "Are you going to keep it or have an abortion?" my sister asks. My sister is single, but she makes a lot more money than me and owns her house, which gives The Checklist of Her Life a higher rating. She is very generous, always pays for my dinner when we go out, sometimes buys me little gifts. She is thinking I can't afford this. My parents are less direct.

"Oh dear," my mother says. "What are your plans?"

"We're keeping the baby," I say.

"Who's *we*?" they ask.

"Me and Bastille," is what I say.

And even though my family is not what I could call happy that I am having a baby, I can tell that in some part of their minds they are a little excited. They start calling me almost every day.

Knowing I am pregnant makes me even more tired. Sometimes when I get home from work, I fall asleep on the couch before eating.

When I finally get up to fix some food, Bastille just glares at me until I take him for his walk. I am too exhausted to do our nightly ritual of me running a comb through his shiny black fur and telling him that tomorrow will be the day that we will finally catch up to a squirrel. And Bastille no longer returns to me when I take him off his leash in the park. He runs from me every time; so there I am, four months pregnant, chasing him around the big old oak trees that line the park path, screaming and begging him to come here.

My mother comes over to help me make the tiny second bedroom, really about the size of a walk-in closet, into a little nursery. We don't know if I am having a boy or a girl, and so we pick the colors pale yellow and white. My mom hangs up a beautiful mobile she bought: silver stars and golden angels floating underneath a cloud. "You loved looking up at the sky when you were little," she tells me as we try to find a way to fit both the crib and the changing table in the tiny room. She never asks me about the father. And once a week my parents show up with dinner and something for the baby. "For the layette" my mother says, and for the first time in years it is easy for my parents to be a part of my life.

My sister goes with me to childbirth classes. I am the only single mother there. The worst class is the first day where they split the couples up (fathers on one side and mothers on the other) and each group had to say what they feared most. I mostly fear the nights, just me and my baby and my dog alone. And that I still have to find day care, not to mention that I will have to pay for it. But what I say is I am worried about something going wrong during labor, which is only partially true.

My friends still call and come by, but I don't go out much anymore. I am too tired and trying to save some money. I know that Neal knows I am pregnant, since it isn't exactly a secret and we have some of the same friends, but he doesn't call even once. One afternoon my friend Renee stops by. She looks great and happy and wants to talk about the baby shower she and my other friends are planning. But instead of feeling good, I am jealous listening to her talk about who is seeing who and what bands are touring and what bands have broken up. I start to do my checklist, adding a category:

social life: none

Renee wants to know what I still need, so I try not to sulk and I think about it. "I could use a stroller," I say. I imagine walking down the street with my baby. The sun would be shining and people would wave. I would be skinny again and it would be Saturday. Then I realize that I have lost Bastille. He is not in my fantasy at all. I try to put him in.

"Maybe you could get me a stroller with really heavy-duty handlebars, so I could walk Bastille too. Or maybe they make strollers you can maneuver with one hand."

Renee looks at me. "What are you going to do about your crazy dog?"

"What do you mean?"

"Well, how are you going to take care of him and all?"

"I just will," I say. But I am beginning to be less certain about my own abilities than I want to be. I wonder how we will get along, Bastille, baby, and me. Not just through long nights of no sleep, but through the days as well.

Bastille is on a leash now, and walks are getting shorter and shorter. One time when we are at the park, he lunges for a squirrel and pulls me down. I don't fall hard, but I have to twist to avoid falling on my stomach and it scares me. "Sorry," I say to my baby. "Sorry," I say to Bastille as I explain why we won't be heading to the park anymore, at least until the baby is born. I put my face against his face and I swear that Bastille knows what I am saying, because he moves away and pulls on the leash all the way home.

That night, I let Bastille out back while I take a bath. As I lie in the tub I can see the baby move around inside me, stretching and shifting. "Soon you will be here," I say and rest my hand on my stomach. At that moment I look up at my bathroom and see the peeling paint, stained porcelain, and a floor that could use a good cleaning. My whole house, really, is pretty shabby. What am I doing? Why do I think I can pull this off?

I get out of the bathtub a little lightheaded and dry off slowly. I look at each part of my body—my hands, my feet, the skin over my belly stretched as tight as the Saran Wrap on the casseroles my mother leaves every week in my refrigerator. I put on my pajamas and practice my breathing. I feel strong. I decide that instead of a stroller, I will ask my friends to sign up on a list to walk Bastille after the baby is born. One more time I will tell Bastille how sorry I am before we go to sleep.

When I open the back door to let him in, he isn't there. So I go outside to the front door and yell for him "Bastille! Bastille!" I scream louder than any women in labor on television doctor shows. I tuck the bottom of my men's pajamas in my boots, put on my coat, and head out. I am both anxious and furious. It is November and cold. "Bastille! Bastille!" I yell. After half an hour of looking I go back to the house and wait.

Finally the phone rings. "Is this Bastille's owner?" a woman asks. When I say yes, she says, "I'm sorry to tell you this, but your dog just got hit by a car. He is out by the curb in front of my house. I think he's dead. I covered him up with a blanket."

"Where are you?" I ask, not even crying, but it is hard to breathe.

I walk the five blocks in my pajamas, and find Bastille lying still on the side of the road, covered in a white acrylic blanket. He is not breathing, but when I touch him he is still warm and doesn't seem to be bleeding anywhere. The woman comes out of her house and stares at me and Bastille for longer than is really polite, then offers to drive us home. She puts newspaper down on her car seat before putting him down.

On my front porch I wrap my arms around Bastille and bury my face in his fur. It is raining lightly and he is damp enough to have his wet dog smell, which is a little like Frito corn chips. I sit there for at least two hours, crying and crying. "I would have left too," I say to him. Finally, I drag him through the house to the backyard, cover him up with his favorite blanket, and go inside. Even though it is after eleven, I call my parents.

"What is it?" my mother asks on the phone. "Are you OK?"

The next day my father comes over and digs a hole in the backyard. My sister brings flowers and some of my friends stop by. Everyone comments on how big I am getting. And when I get into bed, for just one second, I expect Bastille to leap in after me. But he doesn't, of course, and so I close my eyes and think about everything I love about my dog. And I imagine him still running, through the car that slammed into him, past every loud and busy intersection, over every fence, down a long road with a yellow moon and the smell of the Great Lakes getting closer and closer. I lie there wondering how I can feel so full and so empty at the same time. ❧

How has pregnancy affected your way of dealing with loss? What about the way you experience current events? Describe what you feel you have gained and given up during pregnancy. What is the Checklist of Your Life?

Date _____

Womb Dance

Ann Stewart

*B*ig bellies sway and swing. New mothers reach and rock. Young women open and offer. We are wild women dancing.

There are no formal dance steps or techniques. There is no right or wrong. There is only the rhythm, the breath, the body.

We begin the class with walking. "Feel the floor under your feet. Breathe. Feel the ground. Feel your connection to the womb of mother earth," chants our guide Melissa.

At first, we feel self-conscious and move stiffly. Slowly, we allow our awareness to spill down into our elbows. Like liquid, soft and fluid. Appreciating our amazing hands. Breathing into our heart faces.

I am here, five months pregnant with my second child. Dancing the Womb Dance is one of the only times I can be present to this child. My almost-two-year-old toddler fills my days. I wonder how I am going to be present to either of them. How can I divide myself or do I have to? Is there another way to be there for everybody?

We befriend and explore the different energies of birth. By grounding and connecting with all our body parts, we learn to stay alive to the present so that birth can happen. Our dance works with the physical and emotional body through movement.

Melissa starts the music after we have walked and "feel ourselves begin to arrive."

The first rhythm is the rhythm of flowing. The music is gentle, like a lullaby. We practice being both the mother and the child. This is the rhythm of early labor, beginnings, foreplay, the infancy cycle of life. Rocking ourselves. Explore the energy of the egg, learning how to ground and contain. I close my eyes as I undulate to my own rhythms. It is soothing and I feel like I could stay here forever, swaying with my baby.

The music changes. The energy changes—moves into staccato, the second rhythm. The childhood cycle. Active labor. Setting boundaries. Practicing being clear. The father is the teacher. We begin to focus in on birth. Our movements are sharp. Elbows angle. We make edges. The beat is stronger, like African drumming. At first, I don't want the music to change, I am lost to the tranquil moment with my unborn child. But like in birth, the movement comes from my body, not my mind.

My breath comes harder, faster, as I move into the third rhythm—the rhythm of chaos. This is transition in birth, orgasm, the cycle of adolescence, surrender. I try to stay connected and grounded as we give ourselves to the spirit. Birth. I bounce and shake. I feel like a fertility goddess with a huge belly and large pointed breasts.

All self-consciousness has given way to the moment of movement. I'm in a trance, filled with the rhythm of my dance. When the egg and sperm have united, when the baby is born, when something new has been created, there is a release. We are empty and light. The music slows down. I remember the power of my son's birth, the passion and fire of us together. I make a silent prayer that this one will be perfect too. That it will be calm and powerful.

The fourth rhythm is the rhythm of receiving. The maturity cycle of life—when we're mothers, flowing in the juices of all we've let go of and all we've created. The women smile and sway. After we give birth, there is so much room for that which will carry us through the months and years ahead. Allow our joy to fill us, to feed us. Tears flow from my eyes as I fill with the spirit of the Great Mother and the miracle of birth. I am honored to witness it again.

My own dance becomes fluid, connected, and very sweet. I am rocking myself and feel like something greater than myself is rocking me. I hope I can remember this feeling when it's late at night, and I'm holding my new baby. I want to feel the support I feel in this moment, that I, too, am being rocked. I want to hold it in my body and not my mind.

The fifth rhythm is stillness. Our movements are quiet, inward. This is old age in the cycle of life. We are empty. We are full. Awaiting the next wave in the cycle of creation. The music stops.

We come together in a circle of pregnant women. This is a moving practice. Spirit in matter. We are models for other women of what it is to be beautiful, awake, playful, grounded.

I hold my belly, my baby and know I am in practice. I am the Great Mother and I am magnificent. ✽

What is your dance, your most comfortable rhythm; are you tango, blues, waltz? How does your pregnancy fit or not fit into your natural rhythm or dance? How does that fit speak to your image of yourself as a mother? If this is not your first child, how is your pregnancy already affecting the way you mother your present offspring?

Date _____

Science Project

Eugenia SunHee Kim

One evening in March, Jeff and I prepared to document my six-teenth week of pregnancy. It was our weekly ritual—"Jeff and Genie's Science Project." We measured our time in weeks and three-three time: first trimester, second trimester. . . . Each week, we sent a Polaroid to the baby's future godfather in New York. The photos were captioned to highlight a new outfit or to commemorate a milestone such as the first sonogram ("It's a boy!"). Many of the captions referred to my exponential growth.

Unlike my sister who ate a bushel of grapefruit in three days, I had no specific food cravings—any kind of food would do. I ate constantly, since the act of eating was the only cure for my nausea. Thanks to Korean parents, I had small bones and smooth Asian skin. My body hadn't changed much since puberty, until I was thirty-seven and pregnant.

I blossomed so quickly that I was forced to tell my workmates about the forthcoming event weeks before Jeff and I had planned to announce it at our offices. I was a graphic designer for public television and was certain I'd return, after maternity leave, to the supervisory responsibilities and the company and colleagues I cared deeply about. Outside my office door, design staff had posted my image as a multiarmed Hindu goddess. The handwritten subhead read: "I have to do everything around here!" I loved doing everything and being in charge, and pretended to complain about it loudly and often. One day, at the end of a meeting, I said, "Well, somebody had to get pregnant around here."

Telling the news at work seemed to signal to my body that it was now permitted to freely expand. Stretch marks appeared and I wept. I was consoled by shopping with Jeff for a new wardrobe of professional and casual clothes, albeit new big clothes.

It had been a busy work week, and I wasn't feeling inspired about our photo session. Jeff's tie was thrown over a shoulder while he did the dishes. He could wash pots without getting his wrists or cuffs wet. "So what should we do?" he said. He dried his hands and smiled, showing me his big front teeth. They were a pleasing companion to clear blue eyes and the pronounced angles of his jaw and brow.

I tinkered with a pair of chopsticks at the table and spontaneously positioned them like antennae above my swelling belly. "Look."

He took the picture, laughing, "The attack of the alien baby!" He was not far off.

During week 18, my doctor, concerned with my rapid weight gain, sent me to the hospital to test for gestational diabetes. Jeff came with me and even tasted the vile green potion I had to drink, which was the equivalent of a quart of Karo syrup in a six-ounce glass. The test came back positive, and I climbed the salmon-painted concrete steps upstairs to be counseled by a nutritionist. Jeff went back to work, making me promise that I would repeat every word from the session.

My ankles weren't swollen but my upper thighs were bigger than they had ever been, and it was annoying how they swished together when I walked into the nutritionist's narrow office. She was energetic and all business. She was exceedingly slim and smartly turned out in a trim navy blue suit. I hated her.

"What do you usually eat for your meals, Genie?"

"Well, cereal or an egg for breakfast, or toast with cheese and juice. Lunch is a sandwich or yogurt and soup or leftovers from dinner. Then we have chicken or something grilled, rice, and green beans or broccoli or something." Determined to prove how healthily I ate, I didn't mention the cookies, hordes of crackers, or boxes of wheat thins that calmed the churning stomach crowded by the baby-thing growing down there.

She was onto me, though, and launched into a lecture about how important it was for the baby to limit my snacking. She crossed her shapely thin legs, and from a bottom file drawer pulled out plastic food models of all the things I had mentioned, in different sizes. They were grimy from handling and the creamy lumps of white plastic rice made my stomach heave. I swallowed, kept it down.

"Which one of these do you think is a half cup of rice?" She displayed three latex piles of the white stuff. I figured that she focused on the rice because I was Asian. I chose a portion that was typical of what I ate.

"You see? That's actually a cup. *This* is a half cup," and she triumphantly lifted a miniscule pile that I was allowed to eat. She was starting to resemble my worst elementary schoolteacher, and I decided to shut up so I could get out of there without further wounding. I was near tears, but couldn't understand why and refused to let her see them. *Down hormones, down boy*.

She gave me pages of menus and food charts, talking about portion control and how the health of my baby was dependent upon what I ate. I wordlessly accepted her sheets, and she scheduled an appointment in a month to see how I was doing. *As if*, I thought and escaped from her office.

I treated myself to a cab rather than the subway and felt sorry for my gestational-diabetes self all the way home. With the nutritionist's sheets on the kitchen table, I nibbled at four soda crackers I had placed on a napkin by my elbow. I tried to make sense of the menus according to what was in our refrigerator and how we ate, and basically felt bad about being so big and being overbig on top of that. When Jeff came home, he hugged me and said he'd help with portion control and not to worry, it was still early in the pregnancy and I wasn't that far off the correct weight for my time.

For my next two weekly Polaroids, I posed in a houndstooth maternity suit—"Checkered beginnings"—and amongst knee-high tulips in our front pocket garden—"Spring has sprung." In our quiet dark bedroom, with Jeff comfortably snoring inches away, I waited for sleep to arrive and ran my hand over my strange changing body. On the bottom left of my pregnant belly, I felt a protrusion disturbing the smooth curve of the baby yet to come. It didn't feel any different on the inside, but it was odd.

"Hey, Jeff, feel this." I poked him.

"What." He shook himself.

"Look, the baby laid an egg." He turned on the light, and when I saw the concern in his face, I became alarmed. The lump had appeared so quickly and was more foreign than all the other foreignness of pregnancy. I called the doctor in the morning and she saw me first thing. After sonograms and exams, a hernia was diagnosed and surgery was scheduled for the optimal time for a pregnant woman—the second trimester—which I had just entered.

My obstetrician, Connie Bohon, recommended a woman surgeon, Dr. Alley. I was relieved to be surrounded by women professionals during my pregnancy and particularly during this complication. It was like being cared for by my four older sisters. I imagined a basket woven by a soothing web of women's fingers, upon which I could drift peacefully along, as if I was on a river, making a tiny wake by trailing a finger in the water.

On the scheduled day, Jeff took off from work and we drove to Columbia Women's Hospital. I was glad it was the same hospital that I was to deliver the baby in. Dr. Alley met us before we changed into blue garb—Jeff into scrubs, me into the backless, feckless gown I would come to hate. She described the procedure and introduced us to the anesthesiologist, Dr. Lee, an Asian woman. Dr. Lee took my hand and said she would use just the right amount of epidural to prevent me from feeling anything during surgery and to keep the baby from risk.

It was cold in the operating room. The nurses helped me put on elastic knee socks. "For your circulation," someone said. The socks were unbelievably ugly, but ugly didn't matter in this room. They washed me with cold swabs of iodine, did things at my backside, then draped me on the table. I examined the series of lights and pattern of ceiling tile, fruitlessly looking for something that could hold my attention in the view I knew I would be staring at for a while. Lying flat, I felt helpless and out of control.

"When can Jeff come in?"

"Soon," the nurse said. She slid out two flaps on the OR table and strapped my arms on them as if I was going to be crucified. I tried to erase this image by watching the tasks around me. An IV was inserted into one arm. A tented contraption was constructed over my stomach, thankfully obstructing the view. Dr. Lee rolled equipment to and fro, and a fetal monitor was strapped to my belly. I was cold through and through. Jeff was finally allowed in and given a stool next to my outstretched left hand. He sat and we smiled at ourselves in shower-cap-like hair coverings. He gripped my hand in both of his. I felt better.

"Genie?" Dr. Lee said down by my legs.

"Ow." It was a pinprick.

"Few more minutes."

Dr. Alley entered masked and shrouded in blue. I recognized her heavily mascara'd eyes through the plastic shield she wore over them. She reviewed the equipment and the patient. "How are you doing?"

"OK as can be, I guess. Nervous."

"We'll keep a constant eye on your baby. We're doing this at the best possible time. You'll feel some tugging, but we're going to get you good and numb."

"How about this?" said Dr. Lee, still by my legs.

"A thump. That's all."

"Let's give her another minute." Dr. Lee came up and cradled my head. "You're going to be fine. Just let me know if you feel too much discomfort." *Too much*? How much was too much?

Dr. Alley and the two nurses gathered around my middle. The lights above them went on high. I was glad I couldn't see her hands moving. There was a distinct pulling sensation around my left pelvis, as if someone had hooked a line to the bone and was giving it a yank. It didn't hurt like sharp pains or cramps, but it was acutely uncomfortable. I clenched my jaws, wincing. Jeff held my hand and brushed my brow.

"How are you doing?" Dr. Alley said.

"It's like you said, a pulling. It's OK though." I tried to be a model patient.

"Good." She asked the nurse for this or that as she did her work.

The tugging was persistent, which made it worse. They were talking business down there by my belly and I concentrated on holding up to the discomfort. It began to feel as if all three of them had their hands in my gut and were wiggling their fingers around.

"How's the baby?" I said to distract myself.

"Baby's fine. You're doing fine."

"You OK?" Jeff smoothed the wrinkle between my eyes.

Tug. Claw. Grasp. *Stop it! Enough!* I wanted to say. "This is a serious drag," I said. Knowing it would eventually be over, I tried to think about the baby. I stared at a shiny chrome edge of a cabinet. The OR lights reflected in it were like comic-book stars twittering around my head. I had no idea of time passing and worried that I squeezed Jeff's hand so hard his ring might cut into his finger. If I was feeling this much pain, what was the baby feeling?

Dr. Alley said, "I'm getting ready to close you up now, but I want your doctor to see this." *See what?* She said in a low voice to the nurse, "I think Connie's on duty today. Can you have her paged?"

"Is the baby OK?"

"Everything is fine, Genie. You're doing great. The baby's doing fine. Just a few more minutes."

OK. Holding.

The clawing had stopped but the pressure had not. I was freezing. Jeff laid his hand on my forehead and his warmth was welcome. He smiled, but his eyes were serious and worried.

Dr. Bohon entered tying on a mask. They conferred in quiet voices and Dr. Alley said, "I'm going to close you up now and we'll be done." The claws came back and I gritted my teeth.

"Is anything wrong?" asked Jeff.

Dr. Bohon stood by. "Give us a few minutes until she's finished. The surgery is going very well and the baby is fine."

I imagined the alien's tentacles—the alien they found in the egg—playing knick-knack paddywhack on my hipbones. Dr. Alley must be sewing the tentacles down to keep them from harming the baby. There was a flurry of activity at my lower torso and the tugging stopped at last, replaced by a dull soreness. Dr. Alley instructed the nurses about dressings and removed her shield and mask. Her lips were incredibly red and perfectly matched the huge smear of lipstick on the inside of her surgical mask dangling around her neck.

"The surgery went well. You didn't have a hernia after all, so we just closed you up."

"What?" we said.

"You have a uterine fibroid. That's what the lump is. A rather large one."

"It's a benign, fibrous tumor," said Dr. Bohon. "They're not uncommon in pregnancy. This one is in a position that's not harmful to the baby. It's unusual that it protruded in the place that it did, which is why we suspected a hernia. We usually remove the tumors several months after you've had the baby. We can talk about this more after you're rested from surgery."

So it *was* an alien.

Dr. Bohon reassured us in recovery that it was not that uncommon. "Some uteruses react to all the hormones and necessary growth by generating fibrous tumors like this," she said. "They're typically benign, just bundles of tissue. We'll watch you a little more closely, but there's no reason your pregnancy won't progress normally or for you not to have a regular delivery."

I was told to rest for two weeks until the incision healed. The doctor prescribed Tylenol with codeine and suggested ice packs to reduce the use of medication for the baby's sake. My chart was marked "high-risk pregnancy."

Jeff stayed home for the next two days, even though he was new at his firm and also had to study for the bar. He catered to my whims and fancies, and we nested like two expectant birds. An alien had truly entered our blessed event: fear and an unknowable outcome, although all concerned were optimistic. He brought flowers, soup, thick novels, ice packs, and cards from friends. We were more joined in this project than anything we'd attempted in the twenty-two years we'd known each other and the ten years of our marriage. I was sweetly loved and cared for.

The incision healed, the baby grew, and the egg subsided in my expanding uterus. I returned to work and our busy lives continued as before. Memorial Day weekend was coming and we looked forward to a day off and Korean food with family.

The baby was kicking and we could laugh at the alien.

At my mother's house on Monday, we had a picnic in the backyard. Jeff's parents and my three local sisters joined the party, including the grapefruit-eating sister, her husband, and two boys. We'd had our conflicts—English-speaking children in a Korean household—but Mother's Korean food brought us together time and again, especially over the two years since my father had passed away. I was treated like a queen, my throne the one reclining lounger. Mom grilled *bulkogi*, and its smoke and the smells from the table meant family and home— intoxicating in the heat of this early summer day. My nephews screamed and laughed, chasing Mother's scrappy toy poodle. I day-dreamed about what it would be like to bring a baby to such an occasion, and ate well and plentifully, completely ignoring the nutritionist's remonstrations.

After dinner, I didn't feel well and thought I had indigestion, but it was lower and dull. Jeff was worried. The doctor on call said it sounded like false contractions and to have a glass of wine and keep my feet up. The wine was a treat and the remainder of the evening at home was quiet for my belly and me. I went to work the next morning as usual.

By 9:30 I had real cramps and there was blood on my big pregnant-lady underpants. Scared, I called the doctor who said to go straight to the hospital. Her direction had an underpinning of urgency that filled me with fear. This can't be happening, I thought, worried about unfinished work. In front of the PBS building, I sat on the curb crying until Jeff picked me up and we sped to the hospital. The doctor had prepared for my arrival, and I was swept off my feet and deposited in a blue gown in a yellow room in the labor and delivery wing. I was having contractions at 28 weeks.

A fetal monitor was belted to my belly, lubricated with a gel that promoted the transmission of the child's heartbeats to the monitor. Hearing the constant, steady heartbeat of the boy within made him more real, and Jeff and I clung to our intention to give him as much time as possible. They administered Terbuteline by IV, which made my heart race and gave me jitters. I joked about being able to read at the speed of light.

The doctor did a gentle internal exam and found no remarkable dilation. The contractions eased and we breathed a sigh of relief.

"We'll see how you do on this drug and take some tests." The doctor was new to Jeff and me. We hadn't yet gone the full round of having an appointment with each of the eight doctors in the practice, which expectant mothers were required to do since no one could know who would be on duty when the baby came. "Depending on how you react to it," she said, "you may be able to go home on bed rest for the remainder of the pregnancy, or you may have to be monitored more closely on the sixth floor here." That was the wing full of women keeping their legs and fingers tightly crossed. The doctor ordered an EKG and a sonogram.

Throughout the afternoon in the small yellow room, nurses drew blood and technicians brought portable equipment and did their tests.

Jeff made phone calls. The medicine gave me a headache and I was irritable and jumpy. I tried to move as little as possible, finding that stillness helped decrease the contractions. The EKG lady came a second time. We met two shifts of nurses. We listened to the baby's heartbeat.

Dr. Bohon visited us in the evening with test results. We were relieved to see her. In green hospital scrubs with straight, dark hair draped in a loose ponytail, she stood at the corner of the bed where she could see us clearly. "The EKG shows you have an infarct, which means we can't give you the Terbuteline."

"What's an infarct?" I knew what it was, but wanted to be sure I was hearing correctly. My father had three heart attacks before he died of one.

"It's a necrosis, like scar tissue on the heart, that results from having had a heart attack."

"But I've never had one! Could I have had one and not known it?"

"Occasionally, pregnant women give this type of EKG, but we can't take a risk that your heart isn't damaged. Terbuteline is highly stressful. You can probably feel your heart racing. The other drug we can try is magnesium sulfate. The problem with mag sulfate is it might make you nauseous and sluggish and give you headaches. And it's sometimes not as effective as Terbuteline."

"How does it affect the baby?" His heartbeat was a soft thrum in the room.

"The danger to the baby is relative. Naturally anything going into your system will pass through the baby's as well. But the point is to control your contractions to give him the best chance to develop. The drugs going through him are less of a risk than the contractions you're having."

"Whatever you think I should do to help the baby, I'll do." I wasn't being brave. I was afraid.

"I think we'll keep you here in Room 11 until we've got you more stabilized. We'll start on the mag sulfate as soon as we can, and you keep telling the nurse when you have another contraction." She told us more about possible options in the near future, such as putting a stitch in the cervix, and something about as long as the water doesn't break. She said I'd have a cesarean for certain and wanted to know how I felt about it. I had read of the controversy about whether doctors go the cesarean route more often than necessary, but I didn't care—I just wanted what was best for the boy.

They added the magnesium sulfate to the IV drip sometime that night, and everything she said was true. I was deathly nauseous and threw up frequently. Food seemed impossible, but I forced myself to eat for the baby. I had a splitting headache. The contractions were sporadic, but they still came. I was forbidden to leave the bed altogether, since movement, especially sitting or standing up, brought a rash of contractions. I learned how to use a bedpan. Then I found that the contractions were delayed to two hours apart or more if I stayed on my left side. I stayed on my left side. The bed grew harder and harder. The room stayed as small as it was.

It had a window, through which I could see a section of the hospital's brick walls and a trapezoidal hunk of sky. The labor room was hung with curtains in an attempt to be homey. The curtains reminded me of the ones in my mother's kitchen when I was very little. They were cream colored with flecks of red and a pattern of some object I couldn't identify from across the room in bed. When I went up close to my mother's kitchen curtains, the objects turned out to be pans, pot holders, and teakettles. I asked Jeff to inspect the curtain patterns in Room 11. He said they were little flowers. I had hoped they were babies of all colors and sizes; cherubim and seraphim.

Days passed. The heartbeat monitor strummed its comforting beat. Jeff brought books about premature babies. We learned that our boy's lungs were not yet completely developed, which was the biggest risk to having him come out now. They decided I was stable enough to give me shots of steroids to bolster the baby's lung development, but not stable enough to go to a regular room or home.

Luckily, Jeff's office was down the street from the hospital. He came early in the morning to help me sponge bathe, change into a clean blue gown, brush my teeth and comb my hair, which was long and tied in a tangled braid. He brought several breakfasts until we singled out croissants as palatable despite the crumbs. He took his lunch breaks in Room 11 and spent every evening next to me. He fielded visitors and brought gifts. He was my conduit to the outside, and his steady presence was a current of strength and calm upon which I could rest.

I learned how to ask for help, which had always been very difficult. My mother taught us not to make trouble, not to bother others, especially American people. But being immobile forced me to depend on the nurses when Jeff wasn't there. I hated calling them even when the IV alarm went off. Bathroom business was the worst. I was embarrassed and apologized for asking them to bring or remove the bedpan. Everything that went in or out was weighed and measured. I tried to wait until regular rounds of blood pressure and temperature taking to ask for help. It was heaven when a nurse dropped by just to fluff the pillows I was propped up on.

Days passed. I was worried, gagging, and sickly, dulled by the mag sulfate. Whenever a new nurse checked vitals and listened to the baby, inevitably she would say, "Gosh, you're so tiny." These were not welcome words and I hoped it was because they were used to seeing nine-month bellies. My head pounded all the time, like nails behind the eyes. I couldn't sleep. I was allergic to the gel for the baby monitor and the skin on my stomach became itchy and raw. I felt exposed. I ached all over with stiffness, inactivity, and the continuing, unstoppable contractions. My left side was sore. My hair was tangled in oily knots. When I finally said something about feeling so miserable, the doctor allowed occasional Tylenol. I breathed to the beat of the inner boy's heart, and tried to calm my rebellious stomach.

I don't remember the first time it happened, but it happened more than once. The monitor was throbbing its steady rhythm and then it was not. Fetal monitors were also plugged into the nurse's station, probably with alarms, because two nurses rushed in with stethoscopes poised and asked me to turn this way, lift legs, move that way until they found the heartbeat again. It was the sweetest sound, that lub-dub amplified through the swirl of placental water. Frequently, it was because the monitor had slipped off my belly or the baby had shifted. But sometimes it was not. They called them "decels" for decelerations of the heartbeat.

Judy was on duty on the really bad night. She was head nurse and planning on attending medical school. I noticed her proficiency, dry humor, and her gentle hands. I came to adore how she would wrinkle her nose to push up her glasses when her hands were busy. It was late in the evening and Jeff and I were talking quietly in the dimmed room when the fetal monitor went silent. Judy entered, put her stethoscope to my belly and turned the monitor volume up high. I turned as she asked, and then I felt her hands become insistent. Still no sound from the monitor. She called for another nurse and they rolled me around frantically, smearing gel everywhere and searching, searching for the baby's heartbeat, yelling down the hall to get Connie down here stat!— tilting the bed until I was nearly upside down. Jeff stood back to make room and I saw the nurses' shadows cast against the wall, leaping like flames. Then, at last! At long last, a wash of sound hummed faintly through the monitor. Lub dub. Oh God. Getting stronger—joyous sound! I was crying, hanging onto the bed, and the nurses and Jeff were shaking.

Dr. Bohon rushed in and Judy led her to the hallway. That's when I overheard "four minutes certain" and feared the worst for our unborn baby boy.

So fragile was the creation of his life and so primitive were the feats we could perform to help him. What was the test being given here? Why us? Why this baby?

I reached for Jeff and the warmth of his touch reminded me of what he had said so simply a few days ago. Our baby was to be a gift, and we were to be guardians for his well-being. My body was a vessel for his delivery, and I had to turn my head off to my own needs to nourish his. The only thing I could do was to lie quietly still and do nothing.

I couldn't always do it, especially as the days stretched into a week, then more. Dr. Bohon ordered another sonogram to check the baby's position. Based on the frequent decels, they worried that the umbilical cord was wrapped around his neck. It wasn't, but he was in the breech position, feet pointed to the cervix. I was told to prepare for a vertical incision from belly button to pubic bone, which would allow them to open wide the uterus and lift him out with the least amount of trauma.

I was exhausted from constantly feeling awful and holding it in. How much longer could I will my cervix to stay shut? I couldn't concentrate enough to read. Tv didn't interest me. The contractions were increasing in pain if not frequency. I felt my body and spirit slipping into a depression that I couldn't afford. Doses of morphine helped, its golden, soothing tongue spreading liquid balm in my tired pelvis, but I worried about the narcotics and the baby. Dr. Bohon assured me that they just passed through him. I think she could see me weakening. A test model of an electric pneumatic mattress had been delivered to the hospital and she thought the new bed might relieve the pressure of being solely on my left side. It automatically adjusted to fit the contours of the body and was supposed to have massagelike benefits. The air pump was so loud, though, I couldn't appreciate its comfort and after a day, asked for my old bed back. It was harder than I remembered and I realized I missed the dragon sighs of the pneumatic bed's motor, but what could I say after that?

At day nine, a nurse attempted to weigh me. It was more than I could stand. I hated to be moved; it made me rock with nausea. I was sick of throwing up. I was sick of being still. I was sick of bedpans. I was sick of my belly being raw and itchy. She insisted that I be weighed; I hadn't been on a scale since I had arrived. There was a special table for this sort of thing—a bedridden patient—and she had borrowed it from the geriatric wing. I was irritable and crabby and hated being that way. She measured me as if she was fitting me for a casket and then rolled my bed into the hallway where the weighing table was parked. I was in my usual blue negligee and my butt was out in the air. I muttered curses. The table was like a giant version of a supermarket scale. I felt like a piece of meat. When the weighing was over and I was back in bed, I turned down the volume of the baby monitor so I wouldn't have to hear him.

Later that day, I learned that my weight had increased slightly, which was a positive sign for the baby. Jeff said what a good thing it was that I'd been so big in the beginning, because it was paying off now. A nurse came down the hall from the Neonatal Intensive Care Unit and told us how important what we were doing was. She'd seen hundreds of preemies, and knew in intimate detail what they went through if they made it at all. It might not have seemed so, but we were encouraged by her visit. She was a stranger who had heard about us and cared enough to support the endeavor we were submerged in: keeping the baby inside.

Then, the square-fingered nurse with an Irish accent, Bridgette, offered to wash my hair, an enormous treat. In the morning, she told me how much trouble she'd had finding the hair-washing board. It was a stiff rubber mat that supported the neck and shoulders of a patient leaning against a sink. It tapered to a spout at the bottom end. She made me laugh when she said that she signed her third child away to borrow it from the surgical wing. Bridgette had thought hard about how to wash my hair. She put the bed in Trendellenburg, the tilted foot-up position I'd experienced when we couldn't find the baby's heartbeat, and slid the board under my shoulders. She put a large basin on the floor beneath the board's spout. Then she filled several disposable douche bags with hot water and hung them from the IV pole. With their on/off clamps and nozzles, the douche bags were perfect portable waterskins that sprayed warm water with adequate pressure from the force of gravity. I was in bliss.

Jeff came for lunch and rejoiced with me and my clean hair. We wondered at how narrow our lives had become, focused on this one thing, this singular task of keeping the boy in.

On day eleven, I was listless from nausea and strain. The contractions were big. I could only smile when Bridgette told me they had dubbed my room The Genie Kim Memorial Labor & Delivery Room. The evening doctor on duty was immersed in deliveries, and it was a busy night for the nurses. I asked for morphine and it was approved. If I could have tossed and turned, that's the kind of night it would've been. I slept hardly at all.

When Jeff arrived in the morning, I managed a breakfast of croissant and orange juice. I was tired, really tired, and the contractions were painful. He gave me a sponge bath and there was blood from my vagina. We called the nurse, who called the doctor, Nancy Ripp. Jeff described what had happened. Dr. Ripp retrieved the bloodied washcloth from the trash where Jeff had thrown it and gave it a sniff. She did an internal exam. "You're dilated about ten centimeters," she said, snapping her gloves off.

I looked up in alarm, but she was smiling. "How would you like to have a baby today?"

Jeff grasped my hands and I felt a worried relief. I didn't think I could go another hour, but was the baby ready? "Saturday, June 10th," he said. "It's a great day."

Van's struggle in the womb taught me about persistence and patience. From him, I learned about courage. I quit my job and started a freelance business so my time would be more flexible for our son. My business, my pleasure with it, and Van are thriving. At age nine, he takes the bus to a special education school forty minutes from home. He's learning to read and write. He is lyrical, funny, talented, and has the sweetest, most loving nature that could ever be found in a gift such as he is.

The years flip by and the old numbering of weeks has lost its significance. I don't mind this passing, because I have learned that it's not timing, but balance that is everything in a science project such as this. ❧

What has pregnancy made you surrender? How do you feel this will help you to mother? What was your former relationship to your body? What is your current relationship?

Date _____

A Mutual Journey

Belinda J. Kein

Suzanne awakens with a sense of joyous anticipation as if it were Christmas, though it's not. It is well into March and the day of their annual pilgrimage to Jake's parents' house. Her obstetrician has told her that her feelings of anticipation are normal. She has her doubts. She feels anything but normal these days.

Suzanne clambers out of bed, pulls back the shade, and peers out the bedroom window. A bleak white sky jumps out at her. Slick black branches shatter the sky into hundreds of tiny shards. Residual masses of snow slide across roofs like great, lost continents adrift. Icicles hang precipitously from rain gutters. A vague reluctant sun lingers on the horizon. The day promises only more snow. Suzanne yanks the shade down. The day disappears behind it. Jake shifts in bed and pulls the covers over his head. Already she feels her mood falter, her excitement begin to fade like a mirage.

The threat of its retreat sends her on her way. She sheds her pajamas and heads for the shower. Streams of warm water follow the curve of her swollen breasts and circumnavigate her huge abdomen, the tributaries gathering at her navel. She closes her eyes and imagines the baby adrift inside her. She feels that they are on a mutual journey, the end of which grows nearer with each passing moment. She opens her eyes and blinks away the thought. Nine months once seemed like a long, long time. Now it seems like not nearly long enough.

Suzanne climbs out of the shower, shifting her bulk this way and that to maintain her balance. She feels as if disaster awaits her at every turn. She shuffles over to the closet. A heap of clothing grows at the door. She snatches a pair of stretch pants and a blouse and struggles into them. She yanks a comb through her tangle of wet hair, gives up, pulls it back in a lumpy ponytail and hurries, as best she can, downstairs to make breakfast.

At one time, the very thought of food in the morning would have sent her heaving to the bathroom. Today, she is ravenous. Jake's mother always plies them with food, but Suzanne cannot wait. She opens the refrigerator. It is filled to capacity with leftovers, from the anchovies that she ate right out of the can before her horrified husband, to last week's lentil soup that ought to be thrown away. Several items are beyond identification.

She squints into the glare of jars and cellophane-wrapped leftovers. The confusion is overwhelming. She grabs the butter, a carton of eggs, and a jar of wild blueberry jam and shuts the door. The jam is an attempt to hold onto what's left of her waning optimism. It reminds her of summer. Of a time when all of life wasn't muffled by snow.

Suzanne is aware that it's not just the snow. Since the moment she knew she was pregnant, everyone and everything has appeared muted. The whole world is just a foggy notion, out of focus, confusing, distant, beside the point. The only thing that she perceives with any clarity is the stirring child within her womb. A flicker of movement, a tiny bump that moves independent of her, the decided pressure of an elbow or knee, a complete regrouping in search of more room, the accompanying need to pee. Of such things, she is certain.

She puts on some coffee, then fills a saucepan with water and sets it on the stove. The floor creaks overhead. The water comes to a boil. Jake clatters down the stairs and appears fully dressed before her. He is wearing the bowling shirt that his parents gave him. It is gray with bowling pins embroidered on front and back. It's an inside joke. Rarely do any of them bowl. They just like to watch it on television.

Suzanne doesn't get it. The whole thing unnerves her. Noisy, chaotic, unsettling. Those are the terms that come to mind.

"Nice shirt," she says.

Jake smiles appreciatively. "Hey," he says, "We better get a move on."

She reaches for the eggs. "One or two?"

Jake pours himself a cup of coffee and takes a sip. His eyebrows rise quizzically above the rim of his mug, "Huh? Oh." He nods in comprehension, "Two."

She takes two eggs from the carton and holds them above the boiling water, changes her mind and hands them to Jake. "Here," she says, "You do it."

He sets his coffee down on the counter. "Nooo problem," he says. Suzanne cringes as he drops them into the boiling water. One cracks open. Streamers of egg white leak out of the shell into the hot water.

Suzanne lets out a holler and pounds Jake on the arm. "Take it out!" she says. "Take it out!"

Jake grabs her hand. "Hey," he says, "Take it easy." She looks at him as if he'd killed someone. "It's just an egg, for god's sake, Suzanne."

She yanks her hand away. "I know."

He reaches for the bread. "Is it OK with you if I have some toast?"

She gives him a dirty look. "Put some in for me," she says, "Three slices. Raisin." She pours herself a glass of milk and sits down at the table.

Jake extracts his eggs from the water, piles the toast on a plate, and joins her. She averts her eyes as he cracks each egg open and onto his plate. She spreads butter and jam on her toast and imagines it is summertime. She looks up just as he deposits a dollop of ketchup beside the eggs. He swipes at the puddle of yolk with pieces of toast as if he were painting a canvas. Great swirls of red ketchup and yellow egg appear across his plate, on his coffee cup, and along the edge of the place mat beneath them. Suzanne watches aghast. Her stomach churns.

Despite her revulsion, she is still hungry. She considers getting up to get more toast. Peanut butter too. Something smooth and comforting. She pushes back her chair and looks at her rotund belly. She yanks at the waistband of her pants. It is stretched taut and is already well beyond the breaking point. Only a few persistent threads hold it in place. If she gets any bigger, she's bound to explode. She imagines her body flying off in all directions, limbs and organs plastered to the dining room wall. Just picturing it makes her laugh aloud. Her laughter cracks the air. It resembles the shrill voice of something wild. The sound startles her. She looks across the room at Jake to see if he has noticed. He is watching her cautiously, as if she were a stranger.

He eyes her suspiciously. "What's so funny?" he asks.

Suzanne retreats. She shakes her head and waves him away. "Nothing," she says, "Never mind."

He scrapes back his chair, picks up his dish with one hand and slips his other arm around her shoulders. "Come on, babe. Let's have it." He feigns a pout. "I'm gonna feel left out."

Though he's kidding now, she knows that he has been feeling left out lately. The huge swell of her abdomen has grown between them like a wall. Much as she wants to reach out to him, she finds it difficult. Now, she makes an effort to include him and shares the joke. "Oκ," she says, and tells him, letting go a burst of laughter at the end.

Jake's smile fades. He retracts his arm. "That's not funny at all," he says and looks at her as if she's lost her mind.

Suzanne knows that he wants to get close to her and that moments like this don't help. "You had to be there," she says and leaves it at that.

She struggles to her feet. Reaching sideways, she gathers the remaining breakfast dishes. Jake collects the salt and pepper and assorted condiments and shoves them into the cupboard. Suzanne sees him slam the door before anything falls out. That's the way things are these days. They just seem to spiral out of control. She possesses neither the energy nor interest required to maintain any semblance of order. She has a growing sense that anything could happen at any moment.

Suzanne carries the teetering pile of dishes toward the sink. Jake watches wide-eyed as she walks past him, shimmying toward disaster. He reaches out to help her. A coffee mug crashes to the floor. Coffee sludge and clay shards fly in all directions.

Suzanne dumps the rest of the dishes into the sink. "Oh, great!" she says, "Great! Thanks for your help, Jake. Thanks a lot."

Jake remains mute. He grabs a ream of paper towels and sets about mopping up the mess.

Suzanne leans over the sink. She tries not to cry. She squeezes soap over the dishes and turns on the hot water full force. She feels increasing pressure behind her eyes. The water begins to rise. Tears creep down her cheeks and mingle with the rising dishwater. She sobs audibly. Steam billows up and threatens to fill the room. Huge soap bubbles swell until they burst. The water nears the top of the sink. She gazes red-eyed at the spectacle as if she's forgotten why she's there.

Jake reaches past her and turns off the water. He places a hand on each shoulder and pulls her toward him. Her abdomen keeps him at arm's length. "Look," he says, "Forget the dishes." He steers her into the living room, helps her into an easy chair and hands her the Rubik's Cube from the coffee table.

She accepts the offering. One by one, she moves the red, blue, green, and yellow squares this way and that. It's something she's found she has a talent for. To what end, she can't say, but something about it appeals to her. The ease of it, she supposes and the way the squares click neatly into place.

For some minutes, she continues to work the cube. She sings a lullaby, her voice rising with each twist. She has heard that it is good to sing to your baby in utero. She talks to it as well. At night, when Jake's asleep, they have long private conversations. She shares her deepest thoughts with the child inside her. Though the baby can't answer, not in words anyway, Suzanne can feel subtle movements in response to her voice. It's as if the baby understands her completely. She has never felt connected to anyone this way. She wants it to go on forever.

She has secretly named the baby Jonah. Swallowed by a whale. That's how it feels sometimes. Especially when the baby shoves her hard, a little fist or elbow nudging her from within. At those moments she realizes that there's another person in there. An altogether separate person with a will all its own. A person who will fight to the death to get out when the time comes. A person who will grow up and leave her for the chaos of the world. Suzanne has watched her friends do battle with their two-year olds. The prospect is unnerving.

Jake continues to putter noisily in the kitchen. She wonders what is taking him so long. He ought to have finished up by now and, as always, they are running late. Perhaps he is seeking solace in the warm soapy water. Finding pleasure in the completion of ordinary tasks. Enjoying the reprieve from not having to struggle against her.

She considers the possibilities, turning the cube round and round in her hand, before setting it down beside her. She calls to him, but he doesn't seem to hear her. More than likely, that's no accident. Lately, he's begun to tune her out. It's not his fault. She's impossible, and she knows it. Mood swings aside, she can't seem to muster any interest in anything he says. And it's not just him. It's everyone.

Finally Jake walks in drying his hands on the dish towel. "Ready?" he asks.

Another day, Suzanne would have berated him for that and quite possibly for a host of other things. Dish towels are for dishes, she would have said. Now, she bites her tongue and nods as she lifts herself out of the chair. Jake snatches the Rubik's Cube and returns it to its original disorder. "Hey," he says, "Don't forget this." He tosses it in her direction. "Heads up!" She reaches for it. It clatters to the floor. Try as she may, Suzanne can do little more than watch it roll away. Jake picks it up. "Sorry, my fault," he says and hands it to her.

She knows that he is trying to lighten the mood, but her optimism has all but dissipated. She cannot make the leap. She waddles over to the closet, extracts her coat, and slips the cube into the side pocket. She shoves an arm into the first sleeve, but cannot manage the second. Getting dressed has become something of an acrobatic feat.

Jake comes to her aid. "Let me, Madame," he says and yanks her coat-sleeve up and over her arm.

"Hey," she says, "Careful! There's a baby in here." As soon as the words leave her mouth, she regrets them.

Jake lets go of her coat. "Like I could ever forget." He snatches his jacket from the closet and heads out the door.

When she gets outside, Jake is in the truck. He guns the engine. Plumes of smoke erupt in violent bursts from the tailpipe. The truck groans loudly with each burst.

Suzanne picks her way down the icy steps. Here and there she slips, then rights herself. The air is bitter cold. It hurts to breathe. She considers going back inside where it is warm and comfortable and safe.

Jake gets out of the truck. "It's fucking cold out," he says and begins to scrape the ice from the windshield.

She doesn't expect him to offer her a hand. She continues down the walkway, yanks at the door of the truck and climbs in. Jake gets in too. Their breath merges on the windshield. He wipes it away with a gloved hand, buckles his seat belt, and looks over at Suzanne. "Seat belt?" he says. The seat belt barely extends all the way around her. She plucks it to show that it's fastened, then folds her arms over her belly. He puts the truck in gear. "Oĸ," he says, "Then we're off." He steps on the gas and eases the truck out of the driveway and onto the road.

All the way there, the sky remains flat, the roads icy, the truck wavering, uncertain. Still, they press on, anxious to make up for lost time. The world whizzes by, a vast, seemingly infinite blur of snow and bare trees. Sudden gusts of wind push the truck this way and that and threaten to throw it off course. The noise of the engine and the heater make talk impossible and relieve them of the need to speak. For over an hour, they travel in silence, both of them peering into the white expanse beyond the windshield, as if the mere act of keeping their eyes on the road will keep them on track.

Gradually, the white expanse gives way to the vertical thrust of the city. Buildings rush to greet them, then just as quickly pass and disappear. The diffuse white sun, pale and without heat, hides behind one and then another of the brick behemoths that jut out helter-skelter from the horizon.

Suzanne watches warily as Jake guides the truck down one street and then another, between hulking piles of snow and erratically parked and double-parked cars, in search of a parking spot. People honk at random. Occasionally someone yells or curses at Jake or at no one in particular. Jake seems to find it all quite normal, if not entertaining. He grew up on these streets. Its trash-strewn sidewalks and tumbledown buildings served as his playground. Suzanne cannot fathom such a thing. She tightens her arms over her belly.

A car pulls out in front of them. Jake yanks the wheel over and pulls in. He flings away his seat belt. "We're here," he says. Suzanne doesn't move. Jake taps her on the shoulder. "Hey babe," he says, "Time to wake up."

Suzanne continues to stare straight ahead. Jake looks through the windshield to see what she's staring at. The car in front of them looks as though it hasn't been moved in weeks. Piles of snow threaten to obliterate it. A thick wedge of ice grows precipitously from the roof.

"Don't worry," he says with a laugh, "We won't stay that long."

"I want to go home now," she says.

"Come on, Suzanne. We just got here."

"I can't." She shakes her head. "I just can't. Maybe tomorrow."

Jake opens his door. "Look," he says, "We're here. If you want to stay in the truck, fine. I'm going up to see my folks." He gets out and slams the door. She watches him disappear into the building.

Snow flurries begin to fall. Suzanne blinks into the glare as they wend their way down from the sky. Clots form across the windshield. The baby stirs. She looks down at her stomach. The baby seems to be doing somersaults inside her. A huge bump appears off to one side. She wonders if it's his head. Maybe, she thinks, he will be a gymnast. She has seen gymnasts on television, has watched them fly off every which way, far above the earth. The thought scares her. Everyone seems so far away these days.

Suzanne unfastens her seat belt, opens her door, and eases herself out of the truck. Her feet sink and slide in the snow. She finds her footing and gives the door a good shove shut. A small avalanche tumbles from the car in front. Taking heed, she walks with care, planting one foot and then the other in the deep snow, waving her hands about to keep her balance. In fits and starts, she makes her way into the building.

She hesitates, then presses the buzzer. Some moments pass before Jake opens the door. "Surprise," she says.

"Hi," he says and walks off into the apartment, leaving the door wide open and Suzanne outside. Suzanne wipes her feet on the doormat and steps inside, closing the door behind her. She unbuttons her coat. The apartment is warm and smells of coffee. His parents are nowhere to be seen. She pokes her head into the kitchen. Plates of cookies and pastries line the counter. Beside them, the coffeepot gurgles to itself like a contented baby.

Suzanne hears voices coming from the other end of the apartment. They are not the voices of Jake's parents. Intermittently there is a loud crashing sound. She walks through the living room, past a dark wood china closet filled with knickknacks. She recognizes a glass figurine of a swallow that Jake picked out for his folks last Christmas. It is suspended in flight. She wants to touch it, but it looks terribly fragile. Instead, she hurries down the long hallway toward the bedroom.

As she nears the door, the voices and the crashing get louder. She stops just short of the door. No one takes note of her arrival. If Jake is aware that she is there, he is pretending otherwise. He and his parents sit together at the end of the bed. Before them, the television blares. On the screen, people are bowling. Suzanne looks on as men and women in matching outfits toss weighty balls onto the runway. Pins fly off noisily in all directions.

Suzanne slips a hand into her coat pocket and surfaces with the Rubik's Cube. With one eye on the television, she reflexively moves the colored squares into place. The television zooms in. A disembodied voice gives a blow-by-blow description of events. A man hurls a ball down the alley. Suzanne cringes as it crashes into several rows of pins. The pins teeter, fly, and fall about in disarray. The voice grows loud with excitement. The word *strike* is bandied about. There is much applause. Jake and his parents join in.

A huge machine arrives from above. Like a great bird, it lifts the pins, sets them upright, and returns them to their correct order. Suzanne slips the cube into her pocket and removes her coat. She steps into the room and watches wide-eyed as, with each play, the machine swoops down, clears the alley, and returns the scattered pins to their original formation. Though she's seen it before, at this moment the whole chain of events is comforting: the scattering and gathering, falling and righting of pins, and most of all, the inexorable return to order.

She pushes off from the door frame and rights herself. Despite her girth and the coat over her arm, she feels lighter somehow. She knocks on the door frame. "Hi there," she says, "Remember me?"

All heads turn in her direction. "Jake," says his father, "You've been holding out on us. We didn't know Suzanne was here."

His mother moves over on the bed and makes a space between her and Jake. "My, my," she says, "Look at you, Suzanne. You're about to burst." She laughs and pats the bed. "Sit down and take a load off your feet."

Suzanne smiles. "I thought you'd never ask." She totters over to the bed and slips into place next to Jake.

Jake's father reaches forward and turns up the volume. His mother turns it back down. "I can't hear a damned thing," he says.

At that moment, one of the players scores a strike. Pins scatter willy-nilly. Jake jumps to his feet, lets out a holler, then slides back into place. Suzanne feels his momentary absence, the way his weight leaves the bed and returns. She watches the birdlike machine swoop down, sweep the pins away, and magically return them to perfect formation. She looks to either side of her, at Jake and at his parents. The four of them sit together like a row of plump pins, the weight of each sunk deeply into the soft belly of the bed.

Suzanne leans into Jake. He slips an arm around her. The baby shifts, as if seeking its place too. She takes Jake's free hand and places it over her stomach. He moves his hand in slow even circles. She closes her eyes and feels the dual sensation of Jake's hand without and the baby within. Quietly, so as not to startle the moment away, Suzanne hums to herself, to the baby, to Jake, and imagines his hand is a great bird with outstretched wings hovering protectively above the vast swell of her womb. ❀

What new talents have you discovered in yourself through pregnancy? How might they come in handy as a mother? Describe your sense of your baby's personality. Describe or transcribe conversations you have with your baby these days.

Date _____

Mother Tongue:
A Performance Pregnancy Diary

Anne H. Mavor

April

I have just found out that I am unexpectedly pregnant.

I have decided to stop learning Bob's special tai-chi form. It is very rigorous with jumps, spins, and kicks and I was going to perform it and everything. The amazing thing is that I don't especially care that I am disappointing him. I also stopped going into my studio to work. I cleaned up and put all my sculptures and tools away in boxes, but I have no urge to make any more. I prepare to incubate.

May

My incubation period has to wait. I just got an offer I can't pass up. My proposal to present a performance art piece at LACE (Los Angeles Contemporary Exhibitions) was accepted! Yikes! I had totally forgotten about it. They gave me a date in September. I will be seven months pregnant then. Really showing. Can I do it? Do I want to do it? Seven months would be perfect if I wanted to do a piece about pregnancy. There I would be, the great earth mother, the first woman who ever experienced being pregnant. All my insights would be cataclysmic. The audience would hang on every word, every move of my universal belly. Well, I'll think of something. I fired off my acceptance letter.

June

I am still not sure about the theme of this performance. The videotape I sent and the proposal were all about speech and stuttering, my specialty. Can I combine pregnancy and stuttering? After all, they are both about holding something inside. Like a pregnant pause. And then bursting forth with a new idea. In any case, I asked Rouel to accompany me on drums. I have this idea of a song cycle. Songs mixed with stories.

I made myself a costume this week. When in doubt, make a costume, I always say. It is a skintight floor-length dress made out of stretchy fabric. One side is white and the other is black. Sort of an archetypal light versus dark image. It will really accentuate my stomach.

From my notes: Struggling to communicate is like giving birth. . . . Saying a word is creating. . . . We can be pregnant with an idea, waiting for it to be ready to come into the world. . . . A physical effort to say something, a labor . . . I feel blocked on how to integrate personal story with larger picture and nature . . . Life is communication. When we stop, edit, or censor our expression, we stop life.

Some of my working song titles: "Sea Me," "The Wind Lets Me Feel My Skin," "Take It Away DNA," "The Chattering Morse Code That Makes New Life to Order." . . .

All these ideas rumbling around inside me and shooting out. I can't do tai chi very well any more. I'm not even that big yet, but I can't bend down as low. Bob is stumped. But Lakshmi assures me that in Chinese medicine this is normal. Evidently, in pregnant women the energy goes up so that the fetus won't fall out of the uterus. Good idea. I don't want this baby to fall out of me too soon.

July

Every idea I have seems cliché and forced. I keep hearing the audience thinking, wow, she is sure cashing in on her pregnancy! Can't she think of anything else? I am realizing that pregnancy is such a loaded symbol that it will override anything else I do. It's like children on stage. All the attention goes to them because they are giant magnets for all our hopes for the future and unlived dreams. They are also cuter than adults. Will my tummy be cuter than me?

I can't believe it. I never have shrunk from using my body in performance before. All those nude performances. Appropriate nudity, of course. Archetypal characters have been my stock in trade. A ballerina, a mermaid, a chicken hatching out of its egg, a tap dancer, a trapeze artist, a statue of Venus. And now I don't want to share my pregnancy. What is wrong with me?

August

(Direction: use hands to pull these words slowly out of my mouth.)

People think of me as a silent person
I don't feel silent
I talk to myself all the time
Somehow all that talk just doesn't make it to the outside world
I want a perfect moment to be perfect in
I want a perfect package for my perfect thoughts
I want a perfect moment for my perfect package of perfect
    thoughts
Do you have favorite words?
Words that feel good in your mouth when you say them?
Words that look neat?
Words that sound so wonderful you want to cry?
Do you have words that you say only to yourself?

Rehearsals are going well. I have decided to call the piece *Mother Tongue*. It will be a series of songs and stories about stuttering, a musical collage of my experience. I have discovered that it is easy to write songs if I write the words first. They seem to pour out of me. Rouel and I practice a couple of times a week. He patiently teaches me how to stay on the beat. I have decided not to mention my pregnancy at all.

I will, of course, look fabulous. I found the perfect color sequin fabric for the top of my costume. I always wear sequins for my performances. This time it's violet. My top is sleeveless and opens into a circle when I spin around. I already made the pants. They are violet chiffon and make a shushing sound when I walk. With my black high heels I feel like I stepped out of 1955. I also made a chiffon hair thing to keep my hair up. I will glitter.

September

The publicity has gone out from LACE. Here is how they describe my work. "Anne Mavor, who has stuttered since age five, performs *Mother Tongue*, a song cycle for voice and percussion that explores and deconstructs the rhythms, motivations, and meanings of language through repetition, hesitations, and stuttering." Did I write that? I go on Jackie Apple's radio show on Pacifica Station KPFK to promote my performance. I sing one of my new songs but it sounds bland without the drums. I am not scintillating. I can't analyze my work and put it into any historical context. I am just me. No one comments on my big belly and I don't either. I feel invisible.

I am confused by everything. How can I be pregnant like this and still be the intrepid adventurer? How can I ignore this amazing thing going on inside me? I hate it and love it. My big tummy is making the decisions now. The bigger it gets, the more I live in it. Me and my tummy are the entire world and I don't care about anything else.

September 30, 8 P.M. and later

Showtime. I went on second, after a man who read poetry. He took the bus all the way to L.A. from San Francisco just to present his work. I guess he is just as desperate as I am to be heard. I didn't pay attention to him because I was too freaked out about my own performance. I had a respectable size audience. The space was big and bare and the sound bounced chaotically off the walls. My favorite part was the beginning when I stuttered uncontrollably. I performed well, except for a few technical difficulties, like the fact that whenever Rouel played, no one could hear me. The drum set was just too loud and drowned out my wonderful words. Afterward I wandered around among the audience hoping and not hoping that they would comment on my obviously pregnant body.

I wish that my performance had been totally different. If I could do it over, I would gather that audience all around me in a big bunch, close and touching. Then I would sing to them about all my hopes and dreams and how it feels to be me, pregnant. I would not pretend that I was unperturbed. I would not pretend to be an earth mother. I would invite them to make up their own stories about the rest of their lives.

October

The performance is over. I sleep and wait. I go buy a new car. A station wagon. Compared to being in my old vw Rabbit, I am swimming in a huge boat. Me and my big stomach swimming down the freeways.

I don't want to do a performance like that again. It wasn't the topic that was the problem, it was how I did it. Me alone against the audience. Me alone in a big dark space trying to fill it up. Me wobbling on high heels trying to look good. Why do I think that being public means being alone? There must be another way.

November 27

It's almost over. I have just felt the first contractions. But we are going to the Pasadena Doo-Dah Parade today anyway. In fact we are marching in it. Actually I am not marching, I am riding on a float. I am a pregnant Katherine Hepburn on the *African Queen* accompanied by the Marching Leech Kazoo Band. I am wearing a long white dress, a white hat and gloves, and look huge. I have finally fit pregnancy into a performance. No one can miss me. ✵

What costume would you like to wear right now? What float would express your place in the parade? Describe how you are integrating your public and private life as a pregnant person. Reflect on how this may carry over into your dual role as mother and citizen.

Date _____

Chapter Two from *Feather Crowns*

Bobbie Ann Mason

*I*t had been a hard winter, the coldest in Christie's memory. It was too cold for the roosters to crow. Alma beat icicles off the bushes, and the children collected the large ones for the springhouse. When the men stripped tobacco out in the barn, their hands were nearly frost-bitten. The winter wheat was frosted like lace, and the ponds and the creek were frozen solid. Some of the children went sliding across the pond on chairs. Christie couldn't see their fun from the house, but she recalled chair-sliding when she and James were courting back in Dundee and her father's pond froze over. James pushed her hard and fast, and she flew freely across to the other side, laughing loud and wild. That was the only time in her life the pond had frozen solid enough to slide on, but this winter James reported that six cows were standing on Wad's pond.

Amanda had told everybody it would be a hard winter. The persimmons said so, she believed. She broke open persimmon seeds for the children. Inside each one was a little white thing, the germ of the seed. Amanda said, "Look at that little tiny fork. That means a hard, hard winter's a-coming! If it was drawn like a spoon, it would be a sign of mild weather; and if it was a knife, it would mean a lot of frost, but not too thick for the knife to cut. But the fork is the worst."

When James and the boys stripped tobacco, Alma had to wash their smoke-saturated clothes. Christie gazed outside helplessly at the bare black trees, the occasional birds huddling inside their fluffed feathers, and the cows chomping hay beside Wad's barn, making a picture of color against the dusting of snow that had come overnight.

Wad's mercury had gone down to naught on ten different nights that January and February. A snow in early January, after the ice storm, lasted till the end of the month. None of the farmers around had ever seen such weather—but then they always said that, Christie noticed. They'd never seen it so warm, or so cold, or so changeable, or so much rain to follow a cold spell. This year, everybody said the cold winter had something to do with the earthquake that had been predicted for New Year's.

Livestock froze: a cow who freshened too early; then her calf, stranded across the creek; then another cow who was old and stayed out in the storm. Wad and James worked to repair the barn so they could keep the cows in at night. They spread hay for insulation, piling bales in front of some of the largest cracks in the walls. The breath of the cows warmed the barn like woodstoves. Christie felt like a cow inside her tent dress and under the layers of cover on the bed. Her bulk heated up the bed so much that many nights James thrashed himself awake. They couldn't let the fireplace go cold—the children needed its warmth—but Christie felt as if she were carrying a bucket of hot coals inside her. In the past, she had been comfortable with pregnancy because of the privacy of it. It was her secret even after everyone knew. They didn't really know the feeling—a delicious, private, tingly joy. The changes inside her body were hers alone. But this time the sloshing, the twinges, the sensation of blood rushing, the bloating, the veins in her legs popping out—all were so intense it was as if her body were turning into someone else's. Walking from the stove to the dishpan—barely four steps—was a labored journey, her legs heavy like fence posts.

As she grew larger, she felt as though she were trying to hide a barrel of molasses under her dress. She was used to sleeping on her back, but when she gained weight, lying like that seemed to exert enough pressure to cut off the flow of blood to the baby. When she sat, she couldn't cross her legs. Her hip joint seemed loose, and it was painful to bend or stoop or turn her foot a certain way. The right leg seemed

longer, and she walked in a side-to-side motion. She learned to mini-
mize the painful motion, and her right leg grew stiff.

At night, James stroked her belly so sensuously she feared the
baby might be born with unwholesome thoughts. As the season wore
on and she grew still heavier, she retreated from James and wouldn't
let him see her belly. She didn't want him to see the deep-wrinkled,
blind hollow of her navel turning inside out. It made her think of the
apron strings she made by pushing a safety pin through a tunnel of
material and reversing it so the seam was inside. He seemed proud and
happy about the baby, but she didn't think he would care to know that
the baby was kicking—flutters and jabs inside. Men were afraid of
babies. There was so much you didn't tell a man; it was better to keep
things a mystery. One night as she was falling asleep, she felt a sharp
jolt, unmistakably a foot jamming the elastic of her womb. The kick
was violent, as though the little half-formed being had just discovered
it had feet and was trying to kick its way out.

Sometimes a small event would soar through her heart on angel
wings: the train going by, the frost flowers forming on the window
light, flour sifting down onto the biscuit board, a blackbird sailing past
the window in a line parallel to the train. For a moment, then, she
thought she was the blackbird, or that she had painted the frost flowers herself, or that she was setting out carefree and young aboard the
train. One day she heard a flock of geese and went outside bare-headed
to watch them tack across the sky. The lead goose would go one way
and the others would fall out of pattern, and then he would sway the
other way and they would all follow, honking. The stragglers seemed
to be the ones yelling the loudest. She felt like one of those stragglers,
trying to keep up but finding the wayward directions irresistible. It
wasn't just her condition. She had always felt like that. She was hungry at odd times, and she would fix herself a biscuit—cold, with
sorghum and a slice of onion. In the henhouse one day, gathering
eggs, she leaned against the door facing, breathing in the deep, warm
fumes. She cracked an egg against the door and slid the contents down

her throat. Then she laughed, like somebody drunk. Several boys had been drunk and torn up some hitching posts on the main street in town not long ago, she had heard. She wondered what it was like to be drunk. It would probably mean laughing at the wrong times, which she did anyway.

Back before she took to her bed, James had a spell of sleeplessness that made him drag for several days. A farmer couldn't afford to lose sleep, and she blamed herself for waking him up when she got up in the night to use the pot. One Saturday just before Christmas, he had hardly slept all night. He made his weekly trip to town as usual, but he didn't stay long. He came home and slept the rest of the morning. He had never done that in his life, he said, annoyed with himself.

That was the day Mrs. Willy came visiting. Mrs. Willy, who lived by herself in a little white house, lost her husband in a buggy wreck soon after they married. She raised a daughter alone. Now she helped out women and sewed.

"Come in, Mrs. Willy," Christie called. "Clint, get Mrs. Willy a chair. Get her that mule-eared setting chair." But she was in no frame of mind for company. She had ironing to do.

Mrs. Willy stepped across the floor as tenderly as if she feared her weight would break a board, although she was slender and pigeon-boned. Alma had remarked that Mrs. Willy hung around pregnant women like a starved dog around the kitchen door.

She settled down in the chair Clint had pulled out from the back porch.

"Go on out and see if you can help Papper," Christie said to Clint. The other children were gathering hickory nuts with Amanda. James was in the barn rubbing down horse leather.

"I've got a splinter," Clint said, holding up his thumb.

Christie felt her apron bib for a needle she kept there. Holding the boy by the daylight through the window, she picked at the splinter until it shot out. She kissed the dirty little finger.

"I didn't cry," he said proudly.

"Now go on. Papper needs you."

Clint slipped out the back door. Christie had been heating an iron on the stove. She spit on it now to test it. It hissed. She started ironing a shirt.

"I need to do my arning," Mrs. Willy said. She leaned toward Christie with hungry eyes. "What's that baby up to in there today?"

"Growing." Christie didn't want to talk about her pregnancy. She didn't want to satisfy the woman's curiosity.

"And how's your man holding up?"

"He don't sleep good," said Christie, aiming her iron down a sleeve.

"Witches might be bothering him."

"Witches?"

"Here's what you do," said Mrs. Willy, untying the strings of her splint bonnet. "Make him sleep with a meal sifter over his face. When the witches come along they'll have to pass back and forth through every hole in that sifter, and by the time they get done he'll have had enough sleep."

Christie laughed until she had to catch hold of her side.

"Don't you believe that?" asked Mrs. Willy. She was unsmiling, her face like a cut cabbage.

"I can't see James sleeping with a meal sifter on his face," Christie said through her laughter. "Anyway, I wouldn't want witches working in and out of a meal sifter so close to *my* face while I was sleeping. I'd rather be wide awake."

Christie felt her laughter shrink like a spring flower wilting, as Mrs. Willy retied her bonnet strings.

"You've got to get used to waking up through the night," Mrs. Willy said. "That's the Lord's way of getting you used to being up with the baby in the night."

"Does the Lord carry a meal sifter?" Christie asked.

"Why, what do you mean?"

"Oh, sometimes I can't tell witches from devils," Christie said. "Reckon it was witches that made our mule go crazy last summer? And what about that swarm of bees that got after Wad one spring?"

Christie paused to tighten a hairpin. She cast a glance at the ceiling. "And that he-cow that busted out of his stall last week? Witches?"

"Christianna Wheeler!" said Mrs. Willy disapprovingly, realizing she was being mocked. "If you act ill towards people, that baby will have an ill disposition."

"I can handle any witches that get in my house," said Christie, pushing her iron forcibly up the back of the shirt.

"Well, Christie, when you went to camp meeting down yonder at Reelfoot, Alma said you got enough religion to get you through to your time. I hope so."

Christie didn't want to think about Reelfoot. There was a lull, while the fire in their voices died down into embarrassment. Christie finished the shirt and lifted a sheet from the wash basket.

Mrs. Willy said, "You need some new domestic. That sheet's plumb full of holes."

"This sheet's old. I'm aiming to tear it up into diapers."

Christie was glad when the woman left. She made Christie nervous, watching her iron and waiting for a crumb of personal detail. Christie wouldn't tell Mrs. Willy about the particular sensations—the way the blood flowed, the way all those creatures turned somersets in her stomach, the way she jolted awake. One night she had awakened after dreaming that her little sister Susan was alive again. In the dream, Nannie had been tugging on her nipple, but Nannie was Susan. The rhythm of the sucking had words, like words to a song. One of Susan's first words was moo-moo, her word for milk. Awake, Christie remembered the time her mother made a pinafore for Susan, starching the ruffles and working the fine lace. But the dogs tore it off of Susan, chewing it to tatters. Mama had worked on that pinafore for most of one winter.

A few days after Mrs. Willy's visit, James came in unexpectedly from the barn, slamming the kitchen door. He said, "I heard you was nasty to Mrs. Willy."

Christie was standing at the stove, stirring cream corn. "Mrs. Willy?" She turned away from James and reached for a bowl on the shelf. Her heart pounded.

James said, "Her sister's telling how you laughed at her and hurt her feelings."

Christie set the bowl on the table and dumped the corn in it. She said, "Some people like to talk."

For a second James's face looked as hard as clay dirt baked in the sun. "We have to live with all kinds," he said. "You can't just laugh to a person's face, Chrissie."

Christie bent her head down. She was conscious of her swollen breasts, her own, not his or anyone else's. James had never talked to her like this.

"When we moved here, we promised we was going to get along with everybody," he said. "You remember that."

Christie nodded. She was tired. She put her hands on her stomach, and she felt it move. James rarely got upset with her. He usually turned everything into a joke, he was so easy.

"Since you and Mandy went down to Reelfoot, it's like you come back a different woman," James said. "I don't know what's got into you, Christie. You're making my heart ache."

She turned, and her skirt tugged against her middle.

James's face softened a little then. "That baby's coming sooner than we thought," he said, touching her stomach. He seemed shocked to realize her girth.

In bed that night, Christie couldn't get comfortable. She felt monstrously heavy, as if with the weight of opinion. When she got up to relieve herself, she took the pot into the kitchen and tried to hit the side to muffle the sound. Afterward, she reached inside the warming box of the stove for a chicken wing. She gnawed the chicken, then searched for a piece of liver, the grease congealed with the crust. In the dark, she nibbled like a mouse, as quietly as possible, chewing breathlessly. She felt better. She heard Nannie stir on the pallet.

But the pregnancy dragged on, like the winter. Her mother couldn't come from Dundee on account of her bronchitis. And Mama was afraid of the earthquake. Christie had to be helped back to her feet when she sat in her rocking chair. She was afraid of falling. She had to struggle up the steps to the porch. On New Year's Day, she managed to cook field peas and turnip-greens-with-hog-jaws for good luck, but the cornbread burned. She hated being fat. She remembered an old woman in Dundee who told Christie's mother, "I had a fat place to came on my leg, just like a tit." The woman said. "The doctor mashed it up real good and then drawed that fat out through a little hole."

Christie fell asleep early at night, curving away from James. She couldn't sleep comfortably in any position except on her side, with a knee pulled up to support her belly. She curled her body around the baby, holding it as closely as possible—hooked to it from heartbeat to heartbeat, her blood flowing into her child. ❀

What about being pregnant do you keep secret and from whom? What don't you want to share with anyone or couldn't share even if you tried?

Date _____

Openings

Gayle Brandeis

When I was pregnant the first time, my sister gave me a pendant. It was a circle, with a woman figure squatting inside. Her hands were raised over her head, and her birth canal was open—out, to the world; in, to her full, round womb.

I wore the pendant after my son was born, but I felt like I was cheating. My birth canal had not opened. Arin was born by emergency C-section after a scary transfer from the birth center to the hospital. Although I fully dilated, and pushed for over an hour, there was serious fetal distress, and the moment of birth was taken from me. I was unconscious, shut down, when Arin was delivered, and my body was stapled closed.

Three years later, pregnant again, I put the pendant back on. I was determined to have a vaginal birth after cesarean. I knew I could do it, but some scared, scarred, part of me had doubts that my body could open into birth.

Then, my friend Valarie showed up at my door. The sky was beginning to get dark, but the moon was full and radiant.

"We have to go somewhere," she said mysteriously.

I woke up my napping husband so he could watch Arin, and I let Valarie usher me into her car.

"Where are you taking me?" I asked. The street lamps lit up as we passed them.

She just smiled.

I sank back in the passenger seat, my eight-month big belly pointing toward the moon. This is like labor, I thought. You never know where it will take you. I decided to trust the journey, and enjoy the ride.

Valarie stopped the car, and we got out. As we walked across some grass, Valarie began to sing:

"I am opening, I am o-pen-ing . . ."

"This is a ceremony for you," she whispered between phrases. "A blessing way."

By a grove of trees in the distance, I saw a circle of flickering light. Flickering voices joined Valarie in song. I felt like I was entering sacred space. I walked toward the circle on dream legs.

Four women—Kate, Elisa, Debbie, Amy—sat holding candles. I was drawn into the circle. A blanket was wrapped around me. Someone removed my barrette and brushed my hair. My shoes were taken off, my feet bathed in a bowl of warm water and flower petals, then dusted with cornmeal. A wreath of leaves and berries was placed on my head.

A bowl of smoking sage was passed around the circle. Each woman brought the bowl to her eyes, for clear vision; to her mouth, that her words may be true; her heart, for good sharing; her hands, to bless all the hands do; and her feet, that she may walk in a sacred way.

Valarie began to chant—Ya No Ho Wey Ya Ho Wey Ney—Gayle will birth like a bear, she said. Gayle will birth with the strength of a bear.

Together we breathed deep, let deep open sounds come from our throats. Together we drew power from the earth and each other.

Then, one by one, the women came up to me, holding candles. They each gave me a beautiful, heart-made gift, then joined their single candles' flames to the large candle in the center. They took their candles home with them so that when I went into labor, they could light them, to be with me in spirit, to help me blaze through the birth.

My heart opened that night, deep and wide. The Blessing Way, so unexpected, so magical, took me to a place of awe and gratitude. A place flew open so wide within myself, there were no words to express it. We didn't need words.

The opening woman is not honored in our culture. Baby showers are held, gifts are given, but the woman who opens her body is not acknowledged in any meaningful way. The Blessing Way, a Native American tradition, truly honors the woman who opens her body to let life pass through. Traditional baby showers can also be transformed to empower the woman near her birthing time. At my baby shower, each woman brought a bead. Many of the beads had stories behind them: my mother-in-law gave me a bead her mother used to wear, my friend Kate gave me a shell she found on a beach in Baja when her son first weaned. We strung the beads together and created a necklace full of women, full of mother-energy.

One full-moon later, I put the necklace on again. My friends from the Blessing Way lit their candles. The labor was long and hard. I pushed for two hours without making much progress. The baby was stuck at my tailbone, the bone hooked in like a question mark, not letting her pass through. I got to a point where I wasn't sure I could push anymore. I thought I would have to be cut open again, unconscious, stapled shut.

And then, my body opened to the bear. Gayle will birth like a bear. Gayle will birth with the strength of a bear. Suddenly, my tired body was charged with bear muscle. I became the animal. A strength I did not know I had, blossomed from the center of my body.

"The channel's been opened," my midwife said.

When Hannah was born, the birth canal was not the only channel that opened. The channel of my voice, my writing voice, opened as well.

I have always been a writer. I wrote my first poem when I was five years old. After Arin was born, I started making a career of writing. I published my work regularly, but I never had the confidence to embark on a big project—a novel, a book of nonfiction. I didn't think I could do it; completion seemed impossible.

Now, in the four years since Hannah's birth, I have written three novels, as well as a book of nonfiction. The channel's been opened, and words are flowing from my body like the milk that made my children's cheeks plump and radiant.

It's not that I have more time now. I have less. I look at my days with my children, my full-time mothering of children who don't seem to understand the concept of sleep, and I almost can't remember where I found the time to write. In both writing and birthing, the body, the mind, the heart, are burst wide open. We open to let something greater than ourselves pass through.

The day before the Blessing Way, I wrote a poem to psyche myself up for labor. This poem came from my body, and my body remembered it. During labor, it chanted itself through me like a mantra.

We need to dilate to let creativity through, be it in the form of a poem or a baby. The body must be open in order to feel, to love, to birth. When we open our senses, the world enters us, impregnates us with its wonders. If we close our body to experience, our capacity for authentic, fulsome expression diminishes. We become infertile, our creative life barren.

The artist who created the pendant given to me by my sister named it "Receptivity." Receptivity is often thought of as a passive trait, even a sign of weakness. But true receptivity, the capacity to open oneself, to let the world rush in, is a path of power. The open throat can sing a powerful song—of protest, and of praise. The open heart learns compassion and can act toward justice. ✺

What kind of ceremony do you want to affirm your motherhood? What do you want from your friends who are mothers and your friends who aren't? How has being pregnant made you receptive?

Date _____

To a Little Invisible Being Who Is Expected Soon to Become Visible

Anna Laetitia Barbauld

Germ of new life, whose powers expanding slow
For many a moon their full perfection wait—
Haste, precious pledge of happy love, to go
Auspicious borne through life's mysterious gate.

What powers lie folded in thy curious frame—
Senses from objects locked, and mind from thought!
How little canst thou guess thy lofty claim
To grasp at all the worlds the Almighty wrought!

And see, the genial season's warmth to share,
Fresh younglings shoot, and opening roses glow!
Swarms of new life exulting fill the air—
Haste, infant bud of being, haste to blow!

For thee the nurse prepares her lulling songs,
The eager matrons count the lingering day;
But far the most thy anxious parent longs
On thy soft cheek a mother's kiss to lay.

She only asks to lay her burden down,
That her glad arms that burden may resume;
And nature's sharpest pangs her wishes crown,
That free thee living from thy living tomb.

She longs to fold to her maternal breast
Part of herself, yet to herself unknown;
To see and to salute the stranger guest,
Fed with her life through many a tedious moon.

Come, reap thy rich inheritance of love!
Bask in the fondness of a Mother's eye!
Nor wit nor eloquence her heart shall move
Like the first accents of thy feeble cry.

Haste, little captive, burst thy prison doors!
Launch on the living world, and spring to light!
Nature for thee displays her various stores,
Opens her thousand inlets of delight.

If charmèd verse or muttered prayers had power
With favouring spells to speed thee on thy way,
Anxious I'd bid my beads each passing hour,
Till thy wished smile thy mother's pangs o'erpay.

(Wr. c. 1795; pub. 1825)

Are you anxious for your baby to arrive, or are you reveling in the last weeks of your pregnancy? What would you use to coax your baby to enter the outer world or remain inside you a bit longer?

Date _____

Thirty-Six Weeks

Emily Grosholz

Ringed like a tree or planet, I've begun
  to feel encompassing,
and so must seem to my inhabitant
who wakes and sleeps in me, and has his being,
who'd like to go out walking after supper
although he never leaves the dining room,
timid, insouciant, dancing on the ceiling.

I'm his roof, his walls, his musty cellar
lined with untapped bottles of blue wine.
His beach, his seashell combers
tuned to the minor tides of my placenta,
wound in the single chamber of my whorl.
His park, a veiny meadow
plumped and watered for his ruminations,
a friendly climate, sun and rain combined
in one warm season underneath my heart.

Beyond my infinite dark sphere of flesh
and fluid, he can hear two voices talking:
his mother's alto and his father's tenor
aligned in conversation.
Two distant voices, singing beyond the pillars
of his archaic mediterranean,
reminding him to dream
the emerald outness of a brave new world.

Sail, little craft, at your appointed hour,
your head the prow, your lungs the sails
and engine, belly the sea-worthy hold,
and see me face to face:
No world, no palace, no Egyptian goddess
starred over heaven's poles,
only your pale, impatient, opened mother
reaching to touch you after the long wait.

Only one of two, beside your father,
speaking a language soon to be your own.
And strangely, brightly clouding out behind us,
at last you'll recognize
the greater earth you used to take me for,
ocean of air and orbit of the skies. ❦

Did you ever wish you were "everything" to someone: a lover, a parent, a friend? Describe how it feels to be someone's universe now. (A few months from now you may want to refer to this entry.)

Date _____

Conditions

Margaret Willey

*M*ay held the ladder and lowered her belly slowly, watching the water lift the skirt of her maternity swimsuit. The water was warm and she was relieved; she let go of the ladder, turned and fell forward. Chlorine fumes enveloped her; the bleachy smell stirred a childhood memory—Y-Sprites on Saturdays, a swimming class for girls, twelve-year-old May, moored to a corner of the shallow end, watching other, better swimmers. That pool had been small and dim-lit, the tiled walls decorated with leering dolphins, an alien world of impossible tasks. Eight Saturdays. After which she had failed to pass her swimming test; May who never failed.

This pool was Olympic-sized and skylit—a cathedral of a room that muffled all sounds. May pulled herself along the pool's edge, bouncing gently on the balls of her swollen feet. Her belly was weightless; she stared down at it, marveling. When she looked up, she saw two of the older women watching her from the other side of the pool. They were nodding at her approvingly, their heads small and egglike in rubber caps.

"Nice and warm today!" one called. Her bathing suit was as thick and floral as upholstery fabric.

"It is!" May called back. The girlish pitch of her voice surprised her. Other swimmers had trickled in, other gray-haired women. They entered the water one by one in stiff skirts and rubber caps.

The woman who had called out came closer, parting the water with bony arms. "My granddaughter is expecting too," she said. "I've been telling her she should come to the pool with me, but she doesn't swim."

"I can't swim a stroke," May admitted. "My doctor prescribed this for back spasms."

"Oh, it'll help," the woman assured her. "It helps all your aches and pains. None of us ladies here are swimmers. Only our Mr. Timmer." She pointed to the deep end, where a white-haired man was swimming an elegant breast stroke. "We just like to stretch and move around a little. You know. In the water you don't feel so old." She said this as though imparting a secret. "Have fun!" she called, then moved away, back to her friends.

Fun, May thought. It seemed suddenly possible. For the next hour, she circled the older women, returning their approving smiles, propelling her belly back and forth across the shallow end. The baby was kicking, a sensation that seemed, in the water, to be happening apart from her, in another body, pain-free, but still magically hers.

Back at the house, a different wave of fumes met May at the back door. Behind the door, her mother-in-law crouched over a tray of floor wax. "I did your floors," Amanda announced curtly, startling May. "Mind you don't slip."

"The floors?" May repeated. "You *waxed* them?"

"Took me three hours," Amanda said. She lowered herself into a kitchen chair with a muffled groan.

"I hope you didn't overdo it," May scolded. She was angry; wax on her no-wax floors—more trespassing.

"Me, hell!" Amanda exclaimed with a husky laugh. "You're the one who's pregnant!"

Amanda often referred to the pregnancy as a joke someone had played on May, a comeuppance. Her mood soured, May left the kitchen and lumbered into the yard, along the curve of newly landscaped driveway, her lower back tightening with each step. From the mailbox at the driveway's edge, she studied a configuration of new windows across the house's front. Windows were Alan's passion—

arched, circular, bay. The north end of the farmhouse was a study in glass, reflecting the trees and fields that surrounded their remodeled home. Only the back of the house was still primitive and shantylike. *Like me*, May thought, *still the same from behind*. She was carrying the baby high and forward; her narrow back perpetually swayed.

May leaned into the mailbox, closed her eyes and pictured the pool—the shimmering surface, the humid air, the sudden weightless-ness of her belly. All the burdens of her life had briefly lifted. She took it as a sign. The pool was a safe place; spending time there would help her to get through whatever lay ahead—the ongoing invasion of her house, the growing clumsiness of her body, her fear of impending motherhood. She decided that she would go back tomorrow and the next morning—every day, in fact. It was what the doctor had recom-mended, after all.

Amanda had come to the front bay window, a cigarette glowing between her painted fingernails. She would, May knew, complain to Alan later about how thoroughly she had strained her back waxing his floors. She would find a way to mention May's thanklessness. Alan would bring his mother's complaint to their bedroom, presenting it to May with his mix of admonition and apology, entreating her to for-give his ailing mother for her invasiveness, to forgive him for having been blind enough to invite her. They had all miscalculated. May had taken a leave of absence from teaching, trapping herself in the house with Amanda, Alan had invited his mother without first consulting May, and Amanda had come without hesitation.

Poor Amanda, May thought, rubbing her lower hip with the ball of her open hand. *As trapped as I am by Alan's kindness*. She sent her mother-in-law an impulsive wave, one that acknowledged their shared physical frailties. Amanda acknowledged the gesture with a faint nod and the tightest of grins before she disappeared from the window.

"*Every* morning?" Alan asked. "Are you sure?"

"Doctor's orders," May replied.

Alan grimaced, unable to hide his dismay. He knew Amanda would take May's absence personally; she was taking everything personally now.

"It's better for her, too, Alan," May insisted. "She can have the house all to herself this way."

Alan waved her silent; Amanda was returning from the mailbox with the mail, a task she had announced May shouldn't do anymore in her condition. She bustled in, her sandals snapping, and presented her son with a stack of envelopes, proud of him for having received so much mail. The kettle whistled on the stove and Amanda hurried to it, moving through the kitchen with a jauntiness that she saved for the rare mornings when Alan stayed home. She was wearing stretch denim jeans, a checkered blouse tied in a knot at her midriff. The hennaed curls at her forehead were a bright, unnatural red. "What d'you kids want for supper tonight?" she asked Alan over one shoulder.

"Something simple," Alan pleaded.

She beamed at him. "How about a pork roast?" To May, she added, "He loves a nice pork roast. And you could use the protein in your condition."

In their bedroom, Alan defended his mother. "She wants to feel useful. Can't we just let her do the things that make her feel useful?"

"She's teaching me how to be a good wife," May grumbled. "The kind you need, but don't have."

"She's just trying to be my mother again," Alan argued sadly. "Is that so wrong?"

"Is that what it means to be somebody's mother?" May asked back. "Giving the sort of help nobody wants?"

Alan put a hand on her shoulder. "Wouldn't you do as much for your own mother?"

"I would never have invited my own mother," May replied. "And if I had, she wouldn't have come."

Alan looked away. It upset him when May spoke harshly about her long-dead mother. He slid tiredly into his side of the bed, lifted the comforter for May to climb in beside him. "Mom never learned the rules of territory," he said, more to himself. "She never had a house herself."

A parting defense, but for May, one that never failed to pull her back to an earlier promise. May had resolved never to add to the history of Amanda's homelessness, especially once May had left her own state of exile behind.

"She doesn't know what this place means to you," Alan was saying. "She doesn't understand because—"

"It's all right," May insisted. She covered his mouth gently with one hand, then uncovered it and kissed him. "She can have my house. For now. I'll be fine." To herself, she added silently, *I'll take the pool.*

Giggling at her own awkwardness, she tipped from side to side, trying unsuccessfully to float on her back. Finally she rolled over and submerged, crouching under the water's surface with her eyes open. Two pairs of broad hips and wrinkled legs were dancing toward her. It was the same two, and May had learned that they were widowed sisters—Louise and Edna. May surfaced, spouted water and waved them closer.

"Good for you," Edna called. Today she had the sides of her rubber cap curled up; tufts of white hair showed at either cheek. "I was hoping you'd be a regular. Louise and I were admiring your bathing suit."

"This old thing," May said, stretching the peachy front panel over her belly. It reminded her of the suits she'd worn as a girl, ill-fitting, thick-seamed.

"They didn't even make maternity swimsuits when we had our babies," Edna sighed. "Nobody imagined we might want to take a swim, did they, Lou?"

"Shoot!" Louise scoffed. "When I was expecting, I barely left the house!"

"Do either of you have a son?" May asked.

"Three," Edna told her. "And two girls."

"Me, I had all girls." Louise said. "Four in a row."

"Did you ever move in with one of your sons?" May asked. "When your daughters-in-law were expecting?"

"Oh my," Edna said. She exchanged a long, meaningful glance with her sister.

"Only that first time, Edna," Louise pointed out soothingly.

"I'm a fast learner," Edna agreed.

Behind them, Mr. Timmer dove dramatically into the deep end of the pool to begin his laps. He was of a type of slim, long-limbed men whose body is ageless. When his laps were finished, he often helped the more fragile ladies out of the pool. "I wish I could swim like that," Louise said admiringly.

"It's nice just to float around," May said. "So free. Like before I got pregnant."

Edna submerged to her neck and began moving her arms backward in circles. "See this?" she said. "I could no more do this outside of the water than I could fly!"

"Say, do you think we might be getting old?" Louise asked, and the sisters broke into laughter; the sound bounced over May's head, an arc of shrillness above the blue.

During May's second week at the Y, Amanda's cleaning efforts escalated; she moved beyond the floors and carpets, to the closets, the drawers, the tallest cupboards. "Just making myself useful," she would holler from a stepstool as May came in from her swim.

"Don't overdo it!" May would call back. Sometimes even the furniture would be rearranged, and she would make her way through the altered rooms, unruffled by the changes. She felt, as in her first summer with Alan, a detachment, a dreamy confusion about the house's boundaries, mixed now with appreciation of the comforts gained by his remodeling, the airy ceilings, the view out the tall windows, the gleaming floors. In the afternoons, May often sat on the deck at the back of the house, oblivious to the sounds of scrubbing, water running in and out of buckets, kitchen sounds—chopping and scraping, the muffled clanging of her new pots and pans.

She left it to Alan to thank his mother in the evenings. Mother and son would sit side by side in the living room, exchanging the details of their day—Alan the routine dilemmas of the department, Amanda the trials and tribulations of so much cleaning—how it never ended—and the growing list of her terrible aches and pains.

In the pool, Louise told May how much she reminded her of her oldest girl. "Beth was never happier than when she was pregnant."

"Do I seem happy?" May asked, genuinely surprised.

The sisters laughed. Louise exclaimed, "Honey, you're just radiant!"

"Like a Madonna," Edna added.

"It's because of the pool," May said. "On the outside, I barely know who I am anymore."

The sisters exchanged another glance. "Is your mother coming to help you with the baby, dear?" Louise asked.

"My mother died before I met my husband," May confided. "My husband's mother has come instead."

"Oh dear," Edna said.

"Your husband's idea?" Louise wondered.

"He's an only child," May explained. But at the word *child*, she felt suddenly, inexplicably, on the verge of tears.

Edna peered into May's face nearsightedly. "Are you a little upset today?" she asked.

"Maybe," May said, blinking. "Maybe it's hormones."

"Go ahead and cry, dear," Edna advised, backing away to give May a bubble of privacy. "We all have those days once in a while."

And Louise added, "There are plenty of tears in this pool."

❧

After Amanda finished the dinner dishes, she would collapse into a reclining chair, a heating pad pressed to whatever part of her body had been most severely taxed that day—shoulders, knees, neck, lower back. To her son, she complained of headaches, indigestion, allergies. One afternoon her arms broke out into quarter-sized hives from a new cleaning solution; Alan came home early and brought this news to the bedroom. May was sitting up in bed, reading a novel; she put it down and focused on Alan with an effort. Then she said, "Maybe it's not good for her to be here, Alan."

Alan sat down at the foot of their bed. "I don't know what to do! How can I ask her to leave when I'm the one who asked her to come?"

May closed her eyes and pictured the water, luminous and clean around her.

"Stop punishing me," Alan said.

"I'm not."

"You are. Look at you. This is killing me and it's like you're not even really listening."

When May didn't answer, he pleaded, "So I made a mistake, I admit it. Please don't be so cold and distant, I can't stand it, May. Please."

"Give me another week," May requested softly, her eyes still closed. "Another week and I'll come back."

Alan leaned forward gratefully to embrace her, stretching to encompass the mountain of her belly, but she was floating on her back now, her arms open and slack, her chin tipped to the ceiling in the semidarkness.

❧

In the water, she confided, "My husband says I'm cold and distant."

Edna sighed. "Men are no help at all, are they?"

"I promised myself a long time ago that I wouldn't fight with his mother. I promised never to take anything away from her."

Louise insisted. "She knows how you feel."

"A mother can just tell," Edna added.

"But if I ask her to leave," May reported sadly, "he'll never forgive me."

"Oh honey, *he'll* forgive you."

"Will she forgive me?"

"Why should she?" Edna asked, suddenly impatient. "Why should she forgive you?"

She pointed to May's belly. They all three looked at it, as though waiting to see what it would do. May put her arms around it, feeling a rush of protectiveness. Against her arms, the baby hammered and turned.

"I've been thinking," May announced at dinner the following weekend. "I've decided I need to be alone in my house for this last month, before the baby comes."

Under the table Alan squeezed her knee, hard. She ignored him, started again, speaking more directly to Amanda. "You've been an enormous help, Amanda, but what I need now is some time alone to prepare."

Amanda put her knife and fork down slowly, lowered her head, paused before responding. Then she lifted her chin and met May's eyes. Her face had come to life with shock and anger. "Prepare?" she repeated. "Prepare? You're saying that you want me to leave?"

"Yes, that's what I'm saying."

Amanda turned to Alan. "Well, isn't that interesting," she said. "Because I seem to recall a certain phone call where I was told by a certain son of mine that I should drop everything and pack my suit-cases and come five hundred miles to the middle of *nowhere*—"

As she spoke, Alan was saying simultaneously, "Let's not make any decisions tonight, let's all think about what's best before we—"

May interrupted them both, standing up. "This is my decision," she said. "Not Alan's. Mine. And I am sure about it."

A silence fell. In the stillness, May felt energy in the room shift, as though they had all been sucked into another, identical room in a new configuration. Amanda was straight-backed and flashing-eyed; Alan was holding his head; May, still standing, was suddenly dizzy, her knees buckling. The baby shifted too, in a drumroll of sharp kicks; May tipped forward, leaning over the table to steady herself. When she lifted her head, Amanda was also standing, facing her. "I guess maybe I've been your maid long enough," she said. She threw her napkin to the table and left the room.

Alan watched her go, his expression trapped, miserable. "Oh Jesus, May," he groaned. "Did you have to do it like this?"

"You asked me to come back," she reminded him. "I'm back."

"Did you have to be so cruel about it?"

"I'll be a mother soon," May replied. "It makes you cruel."

May was so shaky coming out of the locker-room that even Mr. Tim-mer noticed. He came quickly to the shallow end to help May down the ladder. Then Edna was at her side; she put a papery arm around May's shoulders and led her slowly to the deeper water.

"I swear, honey, you're twice as big as yesterday," she said.

"For heaven's sake, girl," Louise scolded fondly. "Who's the old lady here?"

May sagged into Edna. "I had a rough weekend," she said.

The other seniors came closer, circling her in concern. "Don't even bother to exercise today," Edna insisted. "You just relax. Let the water make you feel better."

Then their arms drew back; they scattered. May wanted to swim after them, to stay close to their limbs and voices. But too much had happened and she was tired.

This would be her last morning swim. She had only a month left and so much to do—too much—rooms to be put back, drawers and cupboards to reclaim. She would need every ounce of her remaining energy. She submerged, cradling her belly, watching from underwater as the seniors began their exercises, a line of disembodied, dancing legs. *Goodbye*, she thought, missing them already, and the pool too, the place where she had briefly been as weightless and unattached as they were, as harmless and unmoored as a girl.❧

Describe something you had to do outside of your comfort level since you've been pregnant or because of it. How has it helped to make you a mother?

Date _____

July

Kathy Casto

The end of things,
summer disappearing into itself,
end of the poppies, honeysuckle,
end of pregnancy, a huge bulb
stuffed with preparation: crib,
bassinet, diapers, tiny gowns, undershirts,
socks, a pair of red shoes,
friends all saying goodbye, one at a time,
as they leave for the mountains or the beach
as if I were going,
as if I were never coming back.

I am afraid of the things that ripen,
berries, flowers, peaches,
my belly hard and stretched,
my navel extruded, the tendons from my ribs
straining from the weight,
the child filling me up,
taking all the room in my bed,
the corners in my house where no one goes,
an elephant in a box,
the fullness of disorder
splitting open,
juice bleeding from a crack in the skin.

This child is ready as a peach,
what I've waited for all year,
what takes my life
and briefly, fully gives itself to me. ❦

*How does the season match your feelings now at the end of your pregnancy? What
are you doing to prepare for birth? What are those around you doing that you
cannot do because you're expecting? How do you usually deal with endings and
beginnings?*

Date _____

Secrets and Dreams

Dawn M. Tucksmith

I dream my baby way before she is born. She exists for a long time in my imagination. I see her and hold her in my arms, my own precious child.

When we conceive, I carry a secret inside me. I am an Amazon protectress, regal, virginal, and pure. Our baby grows and breathes inside me, awaiting the day, months ahead, when she will be born.

I quickly grow heavy, uncomfortable, elephantine. My stomach feels too tight. I imagine the baby as a prisoner longing to break free from me.

I begin to feel a great ambivalence sometimes. It is hard to find the living baby, the verb, in my thoughts; I feel overwhelmed by the article, the noun, *the baby*. I am tired, slow, and always sick. I don't read, write, or even think much.

I have an occasional day when our daughter (we are soon told) does not tie my stomach into knots, weigh me down with concrete in my innards, and turn me into a beast. I feel as light as air these days and walk easily and proudly, a queen.

I pass the halfway mark and the baby begins to just roll and roll in me. She is like a sea. She plays as I fall to sleep; she jumps and dances as I wake in the morning. She becomes a mermaid, a song, a fish, and a bird, but most of all, a dancer. She is nearer, closer, ever more anticipated and real. I love her image, her dream. She grows and I grow with her. I dream her as a toddler, a young girl, a woman, a river goddess, dancing down the earth, somehow still inside me, somehow apart. I begin to wonder about the traits I will pass on to her. Will the pieces of me, inside or out, that I pass on turn into gifts or curses? What are gifts? Blond hair? An artistic bent? A slight mistrust of the world and its inhabitants? A capacity to love deeply but narrowly? There will be albums from me for her to read, and pictures to see. Outfits I will buy with just her in mind. Reciprocal gifts neither of us can know of yet, that will come through the years. She will be the greatest gift I know, one she will give to us, to me.

I am a Hydra now, a sorority sister among other pregnant women, proudly bearing my baby, and also a frozen woman wandering disassociated through her days, just waiting for her baby to be born. I love rocking chairs. Every night after work I collapse into one and fall into a state of arrested animation. My body becomes completely still except perhaps for my toe, pushing and rocking, and my mind calms. I picture myself clasping my baby to my heart on the rocking chair, rocking away with her into a land of dreams and beyond. My baby! Soon I will watch her emerge, a person from the womb. She will grow and develop, continue to emerge, and we will hold and cradle and rock and name her. Yes.

A few more weeks and we will part. She will be one fraction of our small family circle. I know she will enlarge us, and we will change shape to envelop her, but I feel torn at times. I do want her here so badly, but at what cost? As much as I long for her, I regret her coming as well. It will be bittersweet, a new beginning, a larger circle, but an ending to these perfect, clearly defined days as well. We will be whole still, I remind myself. As she has grown from seed to person, I have grown from pregnant woman to mother.

I thank the baby for what she has given me and allowed me to experience. Her turn now.

Ready, our daughter? Let go. ✤

Describe any dreams you are having about your baby. How do these speak to you about motherhood? What is the "shape" of the family you came from, the family you've been a part of during your pregnancy, your family as you imagine it to be in the future? What could you thank your baby for at this point?

Date _____

March 19: Starting Late

Bonni Goldberg

Neighbors appear
in sun-warmed air—
on their lawns and backyards
pull weeds, mow grass,
prune back branches, break and turn
the earth,

bend to plant and seed.
Nine months full, as I walk
by with my pendulum belly,
and each face smiles and nods,
I become Spring.

Twilight, porch light,
my husband and I
inhale cut greens, onion, dirt:
like two old monks at the close of day
composting, even from the waste of our lives,
an abundance. ❀

How has your personal sense of faith been altered and/or challenged by pregnancy?

Date _____

Contributors

Anna Laetitia Barbauld (1743–1825) was a widely published poet and writer whose writings ranged from the highly personal to the deeply political. During her lifetime, she was acclaimed for her poetic genius and talent by Samuel Taylor Coleridge and William Wordsworth. The most current and complete collection of her poetry is *The Poems of Anna Letitia Barbauld* (1994).

Chana Bloch is a poet, translator, scholar, and literary critic. She has three books of poems, *The Secrets of the Tribe*, *The Past Keeps Changing*, and *Mrs. Dumpty*, which was selected by Donald Hall as winner of the 1998 Felix Pollak Prize. She has also published translations of the biblical Song of Songs and the Israeli poets Yehuda Amichai and Dahlia Ravikovitch, as well as a critical study of George Herbert. She lives in Berkeley and teaches at Mills College, where she is W. M. Keck Professor of English and director of the creative writing program.

Deborah Bogen is an award-winning poet and essayist whose work has appeared in *Santa Monica Review*, JAMA, *Mudfish*, and other journals.

Lake Boggan has been a poet for thirty-nine years. Her poems are included in several anthologies, most recently *Between the Leaves*, a collection of writing by booksellers. Ms. Boggan is a manager at Barnes & Noble.

Gayle Brandeis is a writer and dancer living in Riverside, California, with her husband and two children. Her work has appeared in numerous magazines and anthologies and has received several awards. Her books, *Fruitflesh: Living and Writing in a Woman's Body* and

Towards a Center of Voices: Women Poets on Women Poets and the Poetic Process are forthcoming.

Kathy Casto is a poet and on the faculty of the English Department at Portland Community College. Her poetry has most recently appeared in the anthology *I Feel a Little Jumpy Around You*. She lives in Portland with her husband, son, and assorted pets.

Joan Connor's work has appeared in many journals, among them: *Shenandoah*, the *Ohio Review*, the *North American Review*, the *Kenyon Review*, and the *Southern Review*. Her collection *Here on Old Route 7: Stories* is available from University of Missouri Press. She lives in Athens, Ohio, and Belmont, Vermont, with her son, Kerry.

Julie Convisser lives, mothers, and writes in Portland, Oregon. Her poetry has been awarded first prize in the National Portland Poetry Festival and the Oregon State Poetry Association Contest, and has appeared in the *Texas Observer* and several anthologies. She is currently engaged in graduate studies to become a movement therapist.

Chelo Diaz-Ludden has two daughters. She wrote "Evie" in response to her own pregnancies as well as those of others. She has written several short stories and is currently working on a novel.

Rita Dove, former Poet Laureate of the United States, is Commonwealth Professor of English at the University of Virginia. She has received numerous literary and academic honors, among them the 1987 Pulitzer Prize in Poetry. She has published numerous books—her most recent one, the poetry collection *On the Bus with Rosa Parks*.

Carla R. Du Pree, a founding fiction editor of *Shooting Star Review*, finished her master's in The Writing Seminars at The Johns Hopkins University while heavily pregnant with twins and with a two-year-old running about. Her writing has appeared in both anthologies and journals including, *Street Lights: Illuminating Tales of the Urban Black Experience* (Viking Penguin), *Callaloo*, and the *Potomac Review*. She currently teaches graduate fiction workshops at The Johns Hopkins University program in Washington, D.C. She resides in Columbia, Maryland, with her husband, Al, of twenty-two years and her children, The Du Pree Tribe, as she strives to master the balancing act of good, wholesome mothering and getting the ëworkí done.

Hope Edelman is author of *Mother of My Mother: The Intricate Bond Between Generations*, and the international bestseller *Motherless Daughters: The Legacy of Loss*, and editor of *Letters from Motherless Daughters: Words of Courage, Grief, and Healing*. Her articles and essays have appeared in the *New York Times*, *Glamour*, *Self*, *New Woman*, the *Washington Post*, the *Chicago Tribune*, and the *Iowa Review*, among other publications. She lives in Los Angeles with her husband and daughter.

Louise Erdrich lives with her children in the Midwest and is a mixed-blood member of the Turtle Mountain Band of Ojibwa. Her books include *The Beet Queen*, *Love Medicine*, *Tracks*, *The Bingo Palace*, *The Blue Jay's Dance*, *Tales of Burning Love*, and *The Antelope Wife*.

Vicki Forman has received a Pushcart Nomination for her fiction, which has appeared in many publications. Her M.F.A. is from University of California at Irvine, and she teaches creative writing at the University of Southern California.

Molly Giles's first collection, *Rough Translations*, received the Flannery O'Connor Award for Short Fiction, the Boston Globe Award, and was nominated for a Pulitzer Prize. Ms. Giles is an associate professor at San Francisco State University. Her most recent collection is *Creek Walk and Other Stories*.

Emily Grosholz is the author of two previous books of poetry, *Shores and Headlands* and *The River Painter*. She has taught at Breadloaf and the Sewanee Writer's Conference, and is an advisory editor of *The Hudson Review*. She has received grants from the Ingram Merril Foundation and the Guggenheim Foundation. Associate professor of philosophy at Penn State, she lives in State College with her husband, Robert Edwards, and their son, Benjamin.

Amy Halloran is the mother of an eleven-month-old and working on a novel entitled *Church Girls.*

Joy Harjo, a member of the Mvskoke Nation, is a poet and saxophonist. She has published several award-winning books of poetry, including *She Had Some Horses* and *The Woman Who Fell from the Sky.* She also has a CD release with her band Poetic Justice, *Letter from the End of the Twentieth Century.* Her newest book of poetry is *A Map to the Next World*, and forthcoming is a new CD.

Jen Karetnick is a poet and writer in Miami Beach and the happy mom of Zoe.

Belinda J. Kein is published as a poet and short story writer. She recently completed a new collection of stories and is at work on a novel. She has a master's degree in English and teaches community college in Southern California where she resides with her husband.

Eugenia SunHee Kim is an accomplished graphic designer and writer in Washington, D.C. She designs award-winning print materials for educational organizations and international development agencies. She recently received her M.F.A. in creative writing from Bennington College.

Ellen R. Klein lives in New Jersey with her husband, Erik, and son, Sam. Her short stories have appeared in *Fast Fiction 1998.*

Anne Lamott is the author of *Traveling Mercies: Some Thoughts on Faith*, *Operating Instructions*, *Bird by Bird*, and five novels, including *Crooked Little Heart*. She lives in northern California with her son, Sam.

Audre Lorde (1934–1992) published nine volumes of poetry and five works of prose. She was a recipient of many distinguished honors and awards, including the Honorary Doctorate of Literature, Hunter College (1991); Walt Whitman Citation of Merit (1991); Honorary Doctorate of Letters, Oberlin College (1990); Honorary Doctorate of Humane Letters, Haverford College (1989); and the Manhattan Borough President's Award for Excellence in the Arts (1988). She was named the New York State Poet, 1991–1993.

Bobbie Ann Mason has won the PEN/Hemingway Award and was a finalist for the National Book Critics Award, The American Book Award, and the PEN/Faulkner Award. Her books include *Spence + Lila* and *Feather Crowns*. She lives in Kentucky with her husband. Her latest book is *Clear Springs: A Memoir*.

Anne H. Mavor is the author of *Strong Hearts, Inspired Minds: 21 Artists Who Are Mothers Tell Their Stories*. She lives in Portland, Oregon, with her husband, Dennis Karas, and their ten-year-old son, Rowan.

Madeleine Mysko's work, both poetry and fiction, has appeared in journals including *The Hudson Review* and *Shenandoah*. She is the recipient of many honors including a grant from The Maryland State Arts Council, Tennessee Williams scholarships from the Sewanee Writers' Conference, and the 1997 Howard Nimerov Award. She teaches in The Writing Seminars of The Johns Hopkins University.

Kim Nam Jo was born in 1927 in Korea.

Sharon Olds's books include *Blood, Tin, Straw*; *The Wellspring*; *The Father*; *The Gold Cell*; *The Dead and the Living*; and *Satan Says*. Ms. Olds teaches in The Graduate Writing Program at New York University, and for fourteen years has helped run a writing workshop at the Sigismund Goldwater Memorial Hospital, a state hospital for the severely physically challenged. She is currently New York State Poet Laureate (1998–2000).

Anna Purves is a poet and writer living in New York with her husband and son. She is currently completing her novel, *Rights and Desires*.

Barbara Ras won the 1997 Walt Whitman Award for her first book *Bite Every Sorrow* (Louisiana State University Press, 1998). She received the Kate Tufts Discovery Award for 1999. She is also the editor of *Costa Rica: A Traveler's Literary Companion*. She works as an editor for the University of Georgia Press.

Kimberley Evans Rudd lives in Chicago with her husband, David, and three-year-old twins, Victoria Ayanna and Gregory Yohance. A native of Detroit, she cites her mother as her hero. Her freelance writing has appeared in *Essence* magazine, the *Chicago Tribune*, and corporate brochures; this is her first contribution to an anthology. By day, Kimberley creates cause-marketing programs for a national non-profit organization that develops safe playgrounds for children.

Joanna C. Scott is an English/Australian/American currently living in Maryland. Her novels include *Lucky Gourd Shop, Charlie and the Children* and *Pursuing Pauline*. Her poetry has been published in numerous journals here in the United States and abroad, including *Ontario Review* and *The Formalist*. Her awards include *The Lyric*'s 1996 New England Prize for Poetry and The Writer's Voice 1998 Capricorn Poetry Award for her collection *New Jerusalem*.

Rachael A. Silverman is the mother of Isaac and also coordinates homeless services for the city of Portland, Oregon. Prior to the birth of her son, she was a songwriter for and a member of the band Lonesome Taxi. Her songs appear on their CD, *Keep The Change* (which is available at http://www.thespiral.com/store/indies/LONETAXI001 .asp).

Ann Stewart's son Jasper is still dancing along with his new sister Sabrina and his big brother Kyle. Once upon a time, Ann was an outdoor sports writer but her journey into motherhood led her to a career as a parenting columnist, health editor, and freelance writer.

Dawn M. Tucksmith works as a children's librarian in Chatham, New York, where she resides with her husband and three children. She writes short fiction and personal essays. Her work is published in many anthologies and professional magazines.

Suzy Vitello has written a novel and is currently at work on a collection of short stories. She lives in Portland, Oregon, with her husband and three children.

Margaret Willey writes fiction and nonfiction for adults and teenagers. Her most recent young adult novel is *Facing the Music* (Laurel Leaf, 1997). Her story is from a forthcoming collection entitled *Breaking What We Gave Her*.